Blackboard Essentials for Teachers

Build and deliver great courses using this popular Learning Management System

William Rice

PUBLISHING

BIRMINGHAM - MUMBAI

Blackboard Essentials for Teachers

First published: July 2012

Production Reference: 1190712

Published by Packt Publishing Ltd.
Livery Place
35 Livery Street
Birmingham B3 2PB, UK.

ISBN 978-1-84969-292-2

www.packtpub.com

Cover Image by Asher Wishkerman (a.wishkerman@mpic.de)

Credits

Author
William Rice

Reviewers
Robin Hoffman
David Hopkins
Berkley Kilgore
Dr. Malcolm Murray
Matthew Weathers

Acquisition Editor
Sarah Cullington

Lead Technical Editor
Pramila Balan

Technical Editors
Ameya Sawant
Devdutt Kulkarni

Copy Editor
Insiya Morbiwala

Project Coordinator
Sai Gamare

Proofreader
Aaron Nash

Indexer
Tejal R. Soni

Graphics
Manu Joseph

Production Coordinator
Prachali Bhiwandkar

Cover Work
Prachali Bhiwandkar

About the Author

William Rice is an e-learning professional who lives, works, and plays in New York city. He has authored books on Moodle, Blackboard, Magento, and classroom training.

He especially enjoys building e-learning solutions for small- and mid-sized businesses. His greatest professional satisfaction is when one of his courses enables students to do something that makes their work easier and more productive.

His indoor hobbies include writing books and spending way too much time reading http://slashdot.org/. His outdoor hobbies include orienteering and practicing archery within sight of JFK Airport.

William is fascinated by the relationship between technology and society—how we create our tools and how our tools in turn shape us. He is married to an incredible woman who encourages his writing pursuits and has two amazing sons.

You can reach William through his website at http://williamrice.com.

Many of the course materials used in this book's demonstration course are supplied by Open High School of Utah, an innovative and fully online public charter high school that produces quality courses and releases them to the public. Specific thanks goes to the Earth Systems creator and teacher, Jessica Mordecai and to Curriculum Director, Sarah Weston. Learn more at www.openhighschool.org.

About the Reviewers

David Hopkins is a regular blogger on aspects of learning technology, Blackboard, CMS/VLEs, social networks, and other aspects of the utilization of technology in a pedagogic environment. He started blogging about his experiences and activities in 2008, but has been an advocate of blogging and online 'communities' since 1999. His first role was as a web designer.

Using advances in social media and social networks, David has made the most of what is available and has grown an international reputation for his blogging and conference activity. You can follow David on his e-learning blog (www.dontwasteyourtime. co.uk) and on Twitter (@hopkinsdavid), where he writes on the aspects of e-learning, m-learning, pedagogy, learning technology, social media, and social networks.

Berkley Kilgore has been trained by Blackboard to do independent course design. She is a freelance designer who can develop courses in a number of subjects. She received her Bachelor's degree in Ancient History and Sociology, and has worked at American Heritage as the Museum Services Manager. She currently does consulting with them, and is receiving her MBA from the University of Maryland University College.

I would like to thank Elizabeth Kilgore for helping me receive my certification in Blackboard, and keeping my spirits high.

Dr. Malcolm Murray, who was originally a biogeographer based at The University of Edinburgh, Scotland, joined the learning technologies team at Durham University in 2002. He holds a PhD in Geography and a postgraduate certificate in learning, teaching, and research in higher education. He has been a daily user of Blackboard—since Version 5—as a System Administrator, a Building Block Developer, and also at the chalkface to support his teaching.

Malcolm currently leads the learning technologies team at Durham and is an Honorary Fellow of the School of Education. He is a member of the UK Heads of eLearning Forum and Blackboard Idea Exchange. He is also a certified member of the Association for Learning Technology and a Director of **Open Source Community for Educational Learning Objects and Tools (OSCELOT)**. Being a regular presenter at the Blackboard conferences in Europe and North America, he is a past winner of the Blackboard Greenhouse Award (2005), Blackboard Innovators Award (2008), and Blackboard Catalyst Award (2010).

Matthew Weathers is the Applied Instructional Technology Administrator in the Distance Learning Department of Biola University in La Mirada, California. He is also an Adjunct Instructor who has been teaching mathematics and computer science for the past decade or so. His background in the computer industry and his experience in teaching help him train other faculty in the use of Blackboard and other technology on a university campus.

www.PacktPub.com

Support files, eBooks, discount offers and more

You might want to visit www.PacktPub.com for support files and downloads related to your book.

Did you know that Packt offers eBook versions of every book published, with PDF and ePub files available? You can upgrade to the eBook version at www.PacktPub.com and as a print book customer, you are entitled to a discount on the eBook copy. Get in touch with us at service@packtpub.com for more details.

At www.PacktPub.com, you can also read a collection of free technical articles, sign up for a range of free newsletters and receive exclusive discounts and offers on Packt books and eBooks.

http://PacktLib.PacktPub.com

Do you need instant solutions to your IT questions? PacktLib is Packt's online digital book library. Here, you can access, read and search across Packt's entire library of books.

Why Subscribe?

- Fully searchable across every book published by Packt
- Copy and paste, print and bookmark content
- On demand and accessible via web browser

Free Access for Packt account holders

If you have an account with Packt at www.PacktPub.com, you can use this to access PacktLib today and view nine entirely free books. Simply use your login credentials for immediate access.

For Lisa, my loving wife and partner in everything good that I create. And for Liam and Gavin, whose love of learning just for the joy of it inspires me to keep learning.

-William Rice

Table of Contents

Preface   **1**

Chapter 1: The Blackboard Experience   **5**

  Home page   **6**
  Announcements   **7**
  Discussion Board   **8**
  Gradebook   **10**
  Content Page   **12**
  Learning Module   **14**
  Blog   **16**
  Forum   **17**
  Uploaded files   **18**
  Video   **19**
  Wiki   **21**
  Assignment   **22**
  Test   **23**
  Groups   **24**
  Summary   **25**

**Chapter 2: Organizing a Course with Pages
and Learning Modules**   **27**

  Adding Content Areas to hold and organize course content   **27**
    What is Content Area?   28
    How to add a Content Area   28
    What's next?   30
  **Adding a Blank Page tool, which can hold any content
or links that you want**   **30**
    What is a Blank Page?   30

How to add a Blank Page	31
Adding a Blank Page to your course	31
Adding a Blank Page to the Content Area	33
What's next?	34
Composing a page with the HTML editor	**34**
What's next?	36
Creating a sequential path for the student to work through, using a Learning Module	**37**
When to use a learning path	37
How to add a learning path	37
Adding a Learning Module to a Content Area	37
What's next?	42
About the Availability and View settings	**43**
Keeping students informed with Course Tools	**44**
What are Course Tools?	44
How to add Course Tools	47
Adding a Course Tool to the Course Menu	47
Adding a Course Tool to the home page	48
Summary	**48**
Chapter 3: Adding Static Material to a Course	**49**
Adding a file for students to download	**50**
File versus item	50
Content Collections	51
How to add a file	52
Adding an item	54
What's next?	56
Adding a video to your course	**56**
Uploading a video in your course	58
Linking to a video that is on another site	59
Embedding a video on a Blank Page	61
Embedding a video that is hosted on another site	63
What's next?	66
Adding a web link to your course	**66**
Adding a link to an external website	66
Adding a link to a Course Asset	68
Adding an image to your course	**69**
Adding an image to a Content Area	70
Summary	**71**
Chapter 4: Discussion Boards	**73**
About Discussion Boards	**73**
Creating forums with Discussion Board	**74**

Making Discussion Board available to students	**80**
Adding a link to Discussion Board on the Course Menu	81
Creating a link to a forum	82
Managing a forum	**86**
Collecting posts in a forum	86
Grading posts in a forum	90
Summary	**91**
Chapter 5: Blogs and Wikis	**93**
About blogs	**93**
Individual versus class blogs	94
Blogs Course Tool link	94
Creating a blog	95
Making blogs available to students	96
Adding a link to the Blogs page	96
Creating a link to a blog	98
Managing a blog	100
Grading blogs	100
Deleting and editing entries and comments	104
About wikis	**106**
Creating a wiki	106
Adding a link to the Wikis page	107
Summary	**108**
Chapter 6: Assignments	**109**
About assignments	**109**
Adding an assignment	110
Responding to an assignment	113
Summary	**119**
Chapter 7: Testing Students	**121**
Creating a test	**121**
Creating a blank test	122
Determining the behavior of questions by using Question Settings	122
Adding and creating questions on Test Canvas	123
Adding the test to a page in your course	123
Setting the Test Options page	124
Creating questions	**125**
Navigating to the Test Canvas page	125
Enter the type, title, and question text	126
Adding answers and answer feedback	127
Adding categories, keywords, and notes	129

Other types of questions	130
Calculated formula questions	131
Calculated numeric	135
Either/Or—True/False, Yes/No, Right/Wrong, Correct/Incorrect	136
Essay	136
File Response	136
Filling in the Blank and Multiple Blanks	136
Hot Spot	137
Jumbled Sentence	138
Matching	139
Multiple Answer and Multiple Choice	139
Opinion Scale/Likert	139
Ordering	140
Quiz Bowl	140
Short Answer	140
Random blocks versus question sets	**140**
Question pools, the source for random blocks	141
Question sets: fewer limits, greater choices	142
Which should I use: Random Block or Question Set?	143
Creating a question pool	**144**
Creating a random block	**148**
Creating Question Set	**150**
Summary	**152**
Chapter 8: Working with Groups	**153**
Creating groups	**154**
Creating a single group with manual enrollment	154
Creating a group with self enrollment	156
From the student's point of view—self-enrollment into a group	159
Creating multiple groups at once	160
How group settings affect activities	**164**
Sending e-mails to members of a group	**169**
Summary	**170**
Chapter 9: Communicating with Students	
Using E-mails, Messages, and Announcements	**171**
The difference between e-mails, messages, announcements, and alerts	**171**
Sending an e-mail to your students	**172**
Sending messages	**174**
Posting announcements	**176**
Summary	**179**

Chapter 10: Using Collaborate/CourseSites Live **181**

Making your first online meeting a test session **182**
Making Collaborate available to you and your students 184
Launching the Collaborate tool 184
Configuring audio and video 186
Showing a PowerPoint slideshow 187
Using basic whiteboard tools 190
Using the chat 193
Using emoticons during a Collaborate session 195
Talking in Collaborate 196
Taking your students on a web tour 198
Dropping your students on a web page with Web Push 199
Sharing an application on your computer 200
Giving a student the ability to share an application 203
Whiteboarding over a shared application 204
Summary **206**
Before the session 206
During the session 207
After the session 207

Chapter 11: Grading Students **209**

Viewing Grade Center **211**
Finding things that need to be graded 212
Smart Views 214
Creating Grading Periods 215
Creating categories 218
Showing, hiding, and moving rows 219
Some examples of filtering and finding 219
Assigning and entering grades **221**
Screen Reader Mode 221
Manually overriding an automated grade 223
Entering all of the students' grades for an activity 226
Preparing a report for grades **228**
Adding a calculated column 228
Reporting versus downloading grades 228
Summary **229**
Index **231**

Preface

Blackboard Essentials for Teachers gives you all the information you need to build and deliver great courses. The book shows teachers how to construct and deliver a professional quality course using Blackboard's most essential features. The book begins with a tour of a completed Blackboard course. Then you will see, step by step, how to build the example course using Blackboard's free site for teachers — `coursesites.com`.

As you work through the book, you will see exactly how the demonstration course is built. You will see how to add and use interactive activities, media, and other resources. You will also learn how to assess and communicate with students and manage them in groups. You will see how to add static material for the students to view, such as pages, links, and media. Then you will learn how to add interaction to your courses with discussion boards, blogs, and wikis. The book demonstrates how to assess your students with assignments and tests. You will also see how to manage students in groups, and how to communicate with them using messages and announcements. Finally, you will learn the basics of the Blackboard grade book.

What this book covers

Chapter 1, The Blackboard Experience, allows you to tour our demonstration Blackboard course. At each stop on our tour, we will view it from a student's and teacher's role. This will help you learn two things. First, what a teacher can do with Blackboard and second, how decisions made by the course creator affect the student's experience.

Chapter 2, Organizing a Course with Pages and Learning Modules, shows you how to add, remove, and rearrange pages. You will see how to organize course material into learning modules.

Chapter 3, Adding Static Material to a Course, shows you how to add links, web pages, and files to a course. You will learn how to upload your own files, and to use files that other people in your organization have uploaded into the content collection.

Chapter 4, Discussion Boards, shows you how to add and use discussion boards in your course. We'll also look at the capabilities and limitations of discussion boards.

Chapter 5, Blogs and Wikis, shows you how to add and use blogs and wikis in your course. We'll look at the capabilities and limitations of each tool, to help you decide when to use each one.

Chapter 6, Assignments, focuses on creating assignments where the student must submit or upload a file. You will learn how to review and respond to the files that students submit.

Chapter 7, Testing Students, shows you how to add several kinds of questions to your quizzes using Blackboard. You can also add media and descriptive pages. You can control the page breaks in a quiz and create several kinds of feedback. All of these features are covered in this chapter.

Chapter 8, Working with Groups, helps you learn about groups, which enable students to work together. You can create tools and resources, which only the members of a group can access, such as a group Assignment or a group Wiki.

Chapter 9, Communicating with Students Using E-mails, Messages, and Announcements, helps you learn how to send messages to our students, and how to post course announcements.

Chapter 10, Using Collaborate/CourseSites Live, helps you learn about Collaborate, which is Blackboard's application for holding live, web-based sessions with your students. It shows you how to configure audio and video settings, share a PowerPoint slideshow, use the chat feature, share an application, and so on.

Chapter 11, Grading Students, shows you how to use the most often-used features of the gradebook. You will learn how to review the students' grades for your course, including filtering and organizing the display of grades. You will also learn how to associate graded items with a grading period. You will see how to find items that need to be graded, and some options for entering grades. There is a lot to the gradebook, and this chapter gives you a solid start in making the best use of it.

What you need for this book

To use this book, you need only basic computer skills, and a desire to build and deliver the best online courses you can. You don't need any background in online teaching or building web pages. If you are an experienced teacher, you will be able to translate many of the teaching techniques that you use in the classroom, to Blackboard.

Who this book is for

If you are a teacher or a course builder, you need only basic computer skills to get the most from this book. You don't need any background in online teaching or building web pages.

Conventions

In this book, you will find a number of styles of text that distinguish between different kinds of information. Here are some examples of these styles, and an explanation of their meaning.

Code words in text are shown as follows: "Blackboard will plug in values for a and b. It will then calculate c^2."

New terms and **important words** are shown in bold. Words that you see on the screen, in menus or dialog boxes for example, appear in the text like this: "In this example, **Homepage** includes modules such as **My Announcements**, **My Calendar**, **What's New**, and **To Do**".

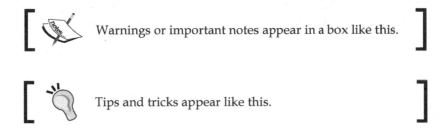

Warnings or important notes appear in a box like this.

Tips and tricks appear like this.

Reader feedback

Feedback from our readers is always welcome. Let us know what you think about this book—what you liked or may have disliked. Reader feedback is important for us to develop titles that you really get the most out of.

To send us general feedback, simply send an e-mail to feedback@packtpub.com, and mention the book title through the subject of your message.

If there is a topic that you have expertise in and you are interested in either writing or contributing to a book, see our author guide on www.packtpub.com/authors.

Customer support

Now that you are the proud owner of a Packt book, we have a number of things to help you to get the most from your purchase.

Errata

Although we have taken every care to ensure the accuracy of our content, mistakes do happen. If you find a mistake in one of our books—maybe a mistake in the text or the code—we would be grateful if you would report this to us. By doing so, you can save other readers from frustration and help us improve subsequent versions of this book. If you find any errata, please report them by visiting http://www.packtpub.com/support, selecting your book, clicking on the **errata submission form** link, and entering the details of your errata. Once your errata are verified, your submission will be accepted and the errata will be uploaded to our website, or added to any list of existing errata, under the Errata section of that title.

Piracy

Piracy of copyright material on the Internet is an ongoing problem across all media. At Packt, we take the protection of our copyright and licenses very seriously. If you come across any illegal copies of our works, in any form, on the Internet, please provide us with the location address or website name immediately so that we can pursue a remedy.

Please contact us at copyright@packtpub.com with a link to the suspected pirated material.

We appreciate your help in protecting our authors, and our ability to bring you valuable content.

Questions

You can contact us at questions@packtpub.com if you are having a problem with any aspect of the book, and we will do our best to address it.

1
The Blackboard Experience

In this chapter, we will tour our demonstration Blackboard course. At each stop on our tour, we will view it from a student role. While looking at the course from a student's point of view, we'll discuss the settings and features that the instructor used, to create what we see. This will help you to learn what you can do with Blackboard. It will also show you how decisions made by the course creator affect the student's experience.

During our tour, we will see many of the features covered in this book, including the following:

- Home page
- Announcements
- Discussion Board
- Gradebook
- Content Page
- Learning Module
- Blog
- Forum
- Uploaded files
- Video
- Wiki
- Assignment
- Test
- Groups

Home page

Our first stop after logging in the course home page:

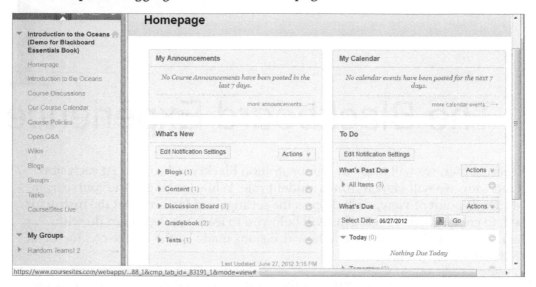

In this example, **Homepage** includes modules such as **My Announcements**, **My Calendar**, **What's New**, and **To Do**. We will take a closer look at some of these modules later. For now, you should know that when an instructor views this page, (s)he will see two buttons at the top of the page, which a student doesn't see — **Add Course Module** and **Customize Page**:

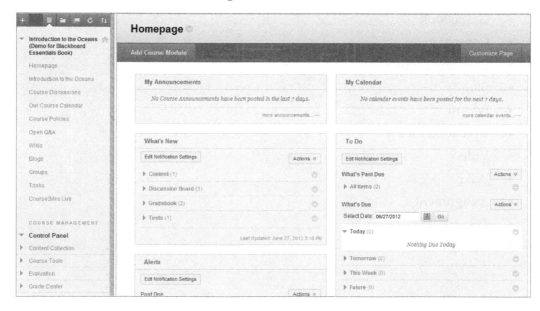

These buttons enable the instructor to add and rearrange the modules on the page. (Your Blackboard system might not allow instructors to use these buttons. If you don't have these buttons, ask your system administrator if you have been given the ability to arrange and add modules.)

Also notice the **Edit Notification Settings** button under **What's New** and **To Do**, and the editing icons in the upper-right corner of each module. These are seen only by the instructor. These extra buttons and icons are a good example of how Blackboard changes the display for students and instructors.

Announcements

Let's take a brief look at **Announcements**:

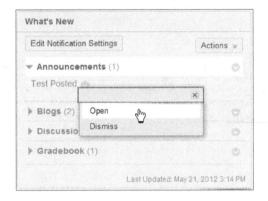

Note that clicking on the arrow icon 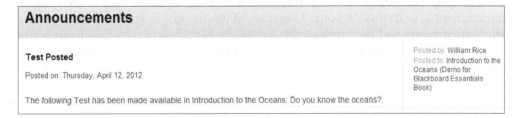 next to **Announcements** displays a pop-up menu. When you want to open or affect an item, Blackboard often places the menu items for doing this, in a pop-up menu next to the item. When you want to manipulate an item, look for the pop-up menu (the arrow icon) next to that item, and if you can't find the pop-up menu, then look in the menu bar at the top of the page.

In this example, clicking on **Open** brought us to the **Announcements** page. This shows all the announcements that the student has received for this course:

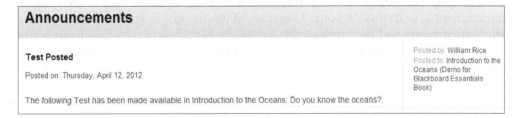

Note that when a student accesses **Announcements** from the front page of a course, the student is viewing the announcements for that course only, and not for any other courses. In addition, **Announcements** are displayed and hidden according to the dates set by the instructor.

You will learn how to use the **Announcements** tool in *Chapter 9, Communicating with Students Using E-mails, Messages, and Announcements.*

Discussion Board

Also within the **What's New** area, we find **Blogs**, **Discussion Board**, and **Gradebook**:

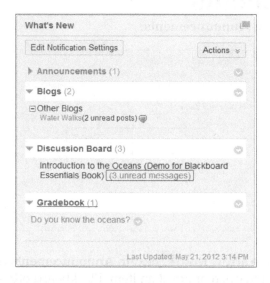

A course can have a blog for all of the students in a course. It can also have a blog for each group of students within the course. And, each student can have his/her individual blog. You will learn more about blogs in *Chapter 5, Blogs and Wikis*, and about working with groups in *Chapter 8, Working with Groups.*

By default, there is a discussion board for a course. Under this board, there are forums. Forums are composed of threads, which are composed of posts written by the course participants. In some Learning Management Systems, there can be multiple forums spread throughout the course. In Blackboard, the **Discussion Board** page puts all of the coursewide forums in one place, as shown in the following screenshot:

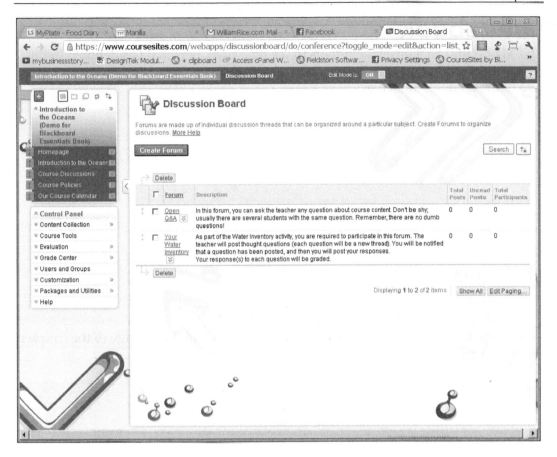

The instructor can add links to the individual forums throughout the course. As a result, the student has two ways to get to the forum that (s)he is looking for. The student can go to the **Discussion Board** page and click on **Forum**, or the student can use a direct link to the forum, which was created by the instructor.

Blackboard offers similar functionalities for blogs and wikis. It collects them all on a **Blogs** or **Wikis** page, and also enables the instructor to add a link to an individual blog or wiki throughout the course.

Gradebook

The **My Grades** tool enables students to see their own, personal **Gradebook**. In this course, in the **What's New** block, you can see that the instructor has recently graded two of the students' activities:

The instructor can also add a link from the student's **Gradebook** page to the course's main menu:

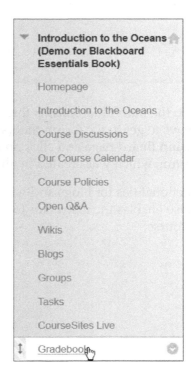

When the student views his or her **Gradebook** menu, the student sees all activities that the instructor has designated as "graded":

My Grades

Item Name	Alignments	Due Date	Last Student Activity	Last Instructor Activity	Grade	Comments
Where did you waste water today?	Alignments		Jan 2, 2012 12:13 PM	May 21, 2012 3:19 PM	1.00/1	Nice comment. It brings up the issue of whether things that truly bring us pleasure are a "waste," and where the line between justified and indulgent is.
Water Walks	Alignments				-/5	
Our Beach	Alignments				-/3	
Take an Inventory of Your Water Usage	Alignments	May 21, 2012	May 1, 2012 2:04 PM	May 1, 2012 2:04 PM	/8	
Do you know the oceans?	Alignments	Jun 6, 2012	May 1, 2012 2:21 PM	May 1, 2012 2:21 PM	10.00/30	
Review Test	Alignments				-/5	
Assignment 1	Alignments				-/10	
Test Average					10.00/30	
Weighted Total					-	
Total					11.00/31	
Weighted Total					-	
Total					11.00/31	
Attitude	Alignments	May 12, 2012			-/5	

Icon Legend

Notice the first graded item, **Where did you waste water today?**. This item is a thread in the forum called **Your Water Inventory**. Blackboard enables you to grade forum postings, blog entries, and wikis. You can use these social tools in your course, and make them part of the grade. When the instructor graded this item, the instructor left a comment, which you can see in the right column of the preceding screenshot.

Note the **Due Date** column for the assignment, **Take an Inventory of Your Water Usage**. This **Due Date** appears on the course's home page, as shown previously in the screenshot of the course home page. The exclamation point in the green box, on this item's line, indicates that the student has finished the assignment and it is ready to be graded. In *Chapter 11, Grading Students*, you will see how to locate only those items that are ready to be graded.

Content Page

Let's move away from the course's home page. The next page we will look at is a Content Page. In Blackboard, a Content Page can hold course content such as PDF files, links to web pages, links to other course pages, and multimedia. It can hold assessments, such as tests and assignments. It can also hold links to activities such as blogs, wikis, and forums.

Our example Content Page, **Introduction to the Oceans**, would be the equivalent of a chapter in a course:

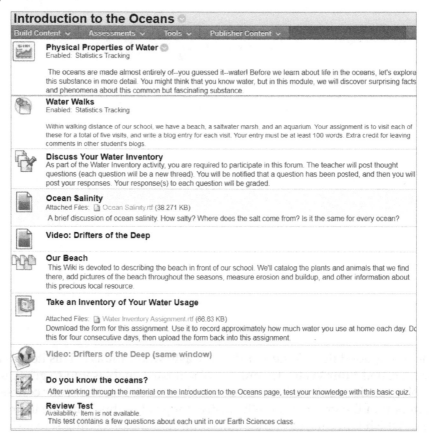

Each of the items on this Content Page demonstrate one of Blackboard's abilities. Let's look at them, one at a time.

Our first item on the page is the Learning Module. It's like another Content Page. You can use Learning Modules to organize your course into units:

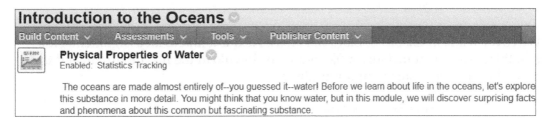

You will learn more about Learning Modules in *Chapter 2, Organizing a Course with Pages and Learning Modules*. Next, we see a link to one of the blogs in the course followed by a link to one of the discussion forums:

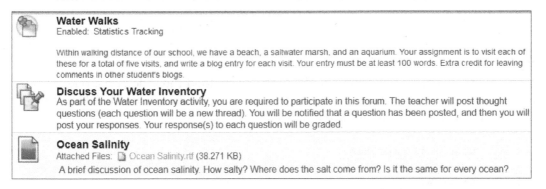

You will learn more about blogs in *Chapter 5, Blogs and Wikis*, and about forums in *Chapter 4, Discussion Boards*. Next, we see two links to files that were uploaded into the course. One is an RTF file, and the other is a video. Note that both of these are files that are now stored inside the Blackboard system, not links to files that are elsewhere on the web:

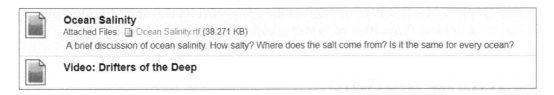

You will learn about adding files to a course in *Chapter 3, Adding Static Material to a Course*. The next item on this Content Page is a link to a wiki in the course:

Our Beach
This Wiki is devoted to describing the beach in front of our school. We'll catalog the plants and animals that we find there, add pictures of the beach throughout the seasons, measure erosion and buildup, and other information about this precious local resource.

We cover wikis in *Chapter 5, Blogs and Wikis*. Next is a link to an assignment. Note that this assignment includes a file. Students download the file, modify it, and then upload it into the assignment for grading:

Take an Inventory of Your Water Usage

Attached Files: ☐ Water Inventory Assignment.rtf (66.63 KB)
Download the form for this assignment. Use it to record approximately how much water you use at home each day. Do this for four consecutive days, then upload the form back into this assignment.

We cover assignments in *Chapter 6, Assignments*. Next, we see a link to a video:

Video: Drifters of the Deep (same window)

This video is hosted on another site. We have embedded the video on a page in our Blackboard course. This is one of the techniques covered in *Chapter 3, Adding Static Material to a Course*. Lastly, we see two tests:

Do you know the oceans?
After working through the material on the Introduction to the Oceans page, test your knowledge with this basic quiz.

Review Test
Availability: Item is not available.
This test contains a few questions about each unit in our Earth Sciences class.

You will learn how to create tests in *Chapter 7, Testing Students*. The first test is a practice test. It won't count toward the students' final grade. You will learn how to include and exclude items from a calculated grade in *Chapter 11, Grading Students*.

As stated before, the first item on this Content Page is the Learning Module. Let's look at the **Physical Properties of Water** learning module in more detail.

Learning Module

In the following screenshot, the student has clicked into the Learning Module. (S)he is viewing a web page that was created and displayed entirely in Blackboard:

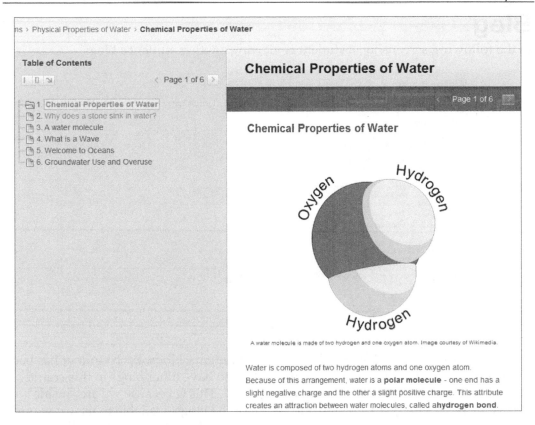

Notice **Table of Contents** for the Learning Module, on the left-hand side of the previous screenshot. This gives the module a level of organization that was missing from our content page.

Also, notice the student viewing the first item in this learning module. The link for the second item has become available. The links for three items and beyond are greyed out, because they are unavailable. In the Learning Module, you can also force the student to view the material in order. This gives the Learning Module a structure that is missing from a simple Content Page.

In general, if you can add it to a Content Page, you can add it to a Learning Module. The Learning Module gives you another level of organization, a table of contents, and the ability to enforce a viewing order for the material. This makes it a good choice for the course material that must be highly structured and learned in a specific sequence.

Blog

In the following screenshot, a student is viewing another student's blog:

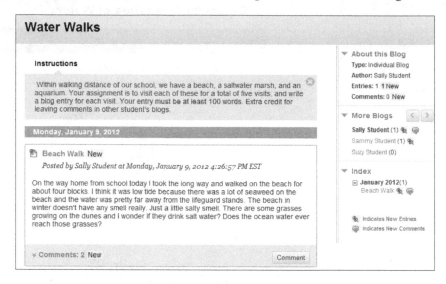

Notice how Blackboard displays links to other students' blogs. Each student has been given a **Water Walks** blog. The students could also have other blogs in this course, but we are not seeing the links to those blogs here. This is because we are "inside" the **Water Walks** blog. If we wanted to see all of the blogs available to us, we would select the **Blogs** page from the course's main menu. The **Blogs** page lists all of the blogs available in this course:

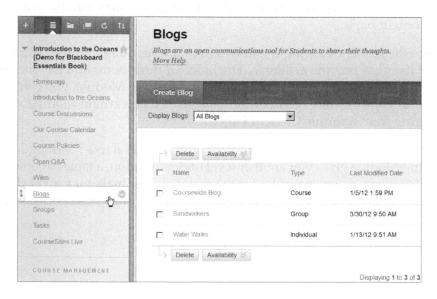

Forum

On the first Content Page of the course, we have a link called **Discuss Your Water Inventory**:

Discuss Your Water Inventory
As part of the Water Inventory activity, you are required to participate in this forum. The teacher will post thought questions (each question will be a new thread). You will be notified that a question has been posted, and then you will post your responses. Your response(s) to each question will be graded.

This link takes the student directly to a forum:

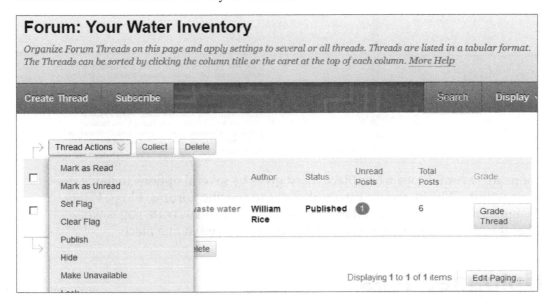

The student could also have arrived at this forum by selecting **Course Discussions** from the course's main menu. This would display a page listing all of the forums in the course, including the one in the following screenshot:

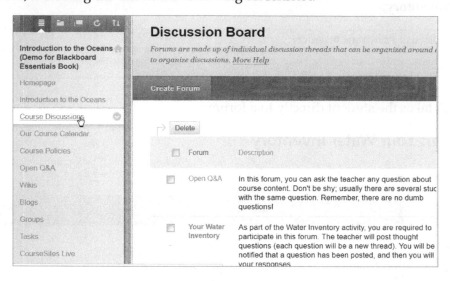

There are several times when Blackboard gives us several options to navigate to an activity. The instructor can create links to specific Forums, Blogs, Wikis, Assignments, and other activities. The instructor can also create pages where all of the occurrences of a type of activity are displayed in one place.

Uploaded files

Further down the page, we see a link to a file that was uploaded into the course. This file is called **Ocean Salinity.rtf**:

Blackboard is in the process of storing this file. However, Blackboard doesn't have an editor or special player for RTF files, that is, it doesn't know what to do with an RTF file. So when the student clicks on this file, Blackboard will not attempt to open it. Instead, the student's browser will "decide" what to do with the file. Depending upon the settings in the student's browser, the file might open in the student's browser, or the browser will ask the student whether to open or save the file, or the file might open in the student's word processor. When you serve a file to the student, you don't have complete control over how that student's computer will handle the file.

Video

Below the link to the RTF file is a link to a video file, **Drifters of the Deep**. This is a web page created in Blackboard, with the video embedded on the page; that is, the page is on Blackboard, but the video is on a different hosting service, such as YouTube or Vimeo:

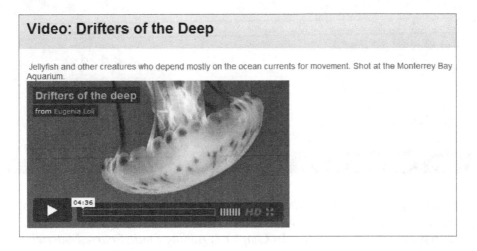

Compare how the embedded video is displayed above, to the one in the following screenshot:

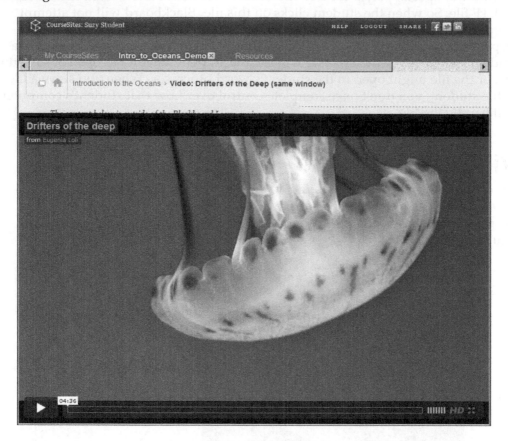

In this example, we uploaded the video file into Blackboard. The file is no longer being stored and played on an external site. Blackboard is using its built-in media player to display and play the file. In *Chapter 3, Adding Static Course Material*, you will see how to add a video by embedding it on a page and uploading it into your course.

Wiki

In the following screenshot, the student is viewing a wiki:

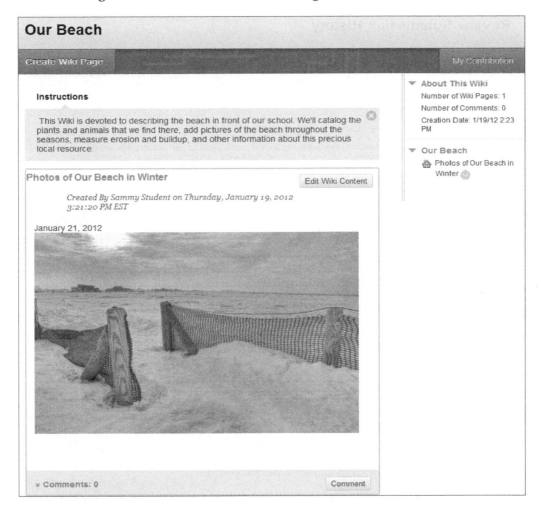

Just like a course can have several blogs and forums, a course can have several wikis. And just like the forums are collected on the Discussion Board page, the wikis are collected on the Wiki page.

The buttons that are displayed on this Wiki page indicate that the student can edit the content and leave comments. You can control whether the students can edit and comment on a wiki. You'll learn more about them in *Chapter 5, Blogs and Wikis*.

Assignment

In the following screenshot, the student is viewing an assignment:

Notice that the student has already uploaded her answers to this assignment. You can see that under **Review Submission History**. However, the **Start New Submission** button enables her to submit another version of her work. You can control whether students get multiple attempts at an assignment. The number of attempts allowed is one of the features we'll cover in *Chapter 6, Assignments*.

Test

In the following screenshot, the student is viewing a test:

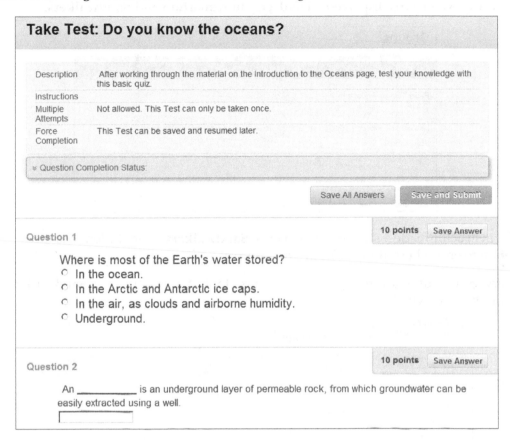

Notice the notes at the top of the page, for **Multiple Attempts** and **Force Completion**. These are settings that the instructor can control. In this example, the test counts towards the student's grade, so the instructor allows only one attempt. If this were a practice test, the instructor could allow unlimited attempts and exclude the test from the gradebook. You will learn more about this in *Chapter 7, Tests*.

Groups

In the following screenshot, the student is viewing the **Groups** page. Note that there are two groups displayed—**Field Trip to Aquarium** and **Sandwalkers**.

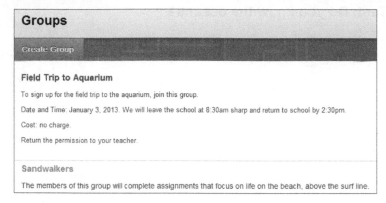

The instructor made a student a member of **Sandwalkers**. This student has the option to enroll herself in the Field Trip group as well.

Every group automatically gets its own course tools; for example, the **Sandwalkers** group has its own blog:

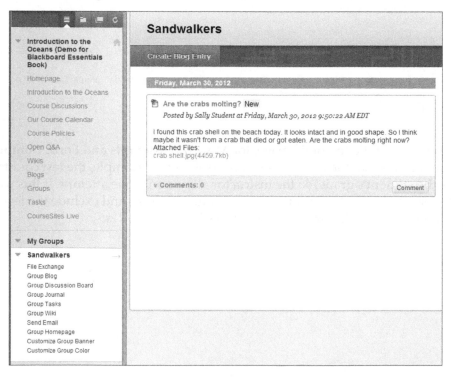

In some cases, group activities are visible to everyone in the course. In other cases, group activities are visible only to members of the specified group. You will learn about these settings in *Chapter 8, Working with Groups.*

A group activity, like the blog shown previously, can be graded. When you give a grade for a group activity, everyone in the specified group gets the same grade.

Summary

In this chapter, we toured the demonstration course that we will create in this book. The course uses Blackboard's core features. There are many other features and settings available to you. The ones discussed in this chapter will enable you to create an effective, engaging course.

Now, let's get started with building our course.

2
Organizing a Course with Pages and Learning Modules

Blackboard enables you to add different types of pages to a course. Each type of page adds different kinds of functionality to your course. This chapter shows you how to add, remove, and rearrange pages. You will see how to organize course material into Learning Modules. In the next chapter, you will populate the Pages and Learning Modules with static course material.

In this chapter, you will be learning how to do the following:

- Adding Content Areas to hold and organize course content
- Adding a Blank Page tool, which can hold any content, or links that you want
- Understanding the difference between a Blank Page and a Content Page, and when to use each
- Creating a sequential path for the student to work through, using a Learning Module
- Adding links to useful tools, such as the course glossary, calendar, or messages

Adding Content Areas to hold and organize course content

In Blackboard, **Content Area** is intended to be used like a topic or chapter. Of course, you can have as many or as few Content Areas as you want in a course. You can even build a course without using the Content Area tool. In our demonstration, we will use the Content Area tool in the most common way, that is, to organize our course into topics, with one topic per Content Area.

What is Content Area?

In Blackboard, Content Area is a special kind of course page. Adding Content Area adds a link to the Course Menu. In a Content Area, you can add many kinds of course material, activities, and tools.

Usually, we add a Content Area for each topic or chapter in a course. Use a Content Area when you want to add different kinds of resources and activities to a topic, such as links, graphics, videos, tests, assignments, surveys, and more.

How to add a Content Area

In this chapter, we will cover how to add a Content Area. In other chapters, we will cover how to add items to a Content Area.

To add a Content Area, perform the following steps:

1. In the upper-right corner of the page, ensure that **Edit Mode is:** is set to **ON**:

2. From **Course Menu**, select **Create Content Area**:

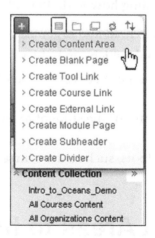

3. Blackboard will prompt you to name the Content Area. The **Name:** field that you enter here will be displayed as a link in the Course Menu, and in a tab across the top of the course window:

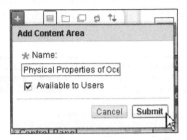

4. If you select **Available to Users**, students in this course will be able to see the Content Area. If you do not make it available, it will be hidden from the students, and the link and tab for this Content Area will not appear.

Hide Content Areas to keep them in reserve, just in case

You can create Content Areas and keep them hidden in your course until you need them. Extra-credit activities, assignments that you might not have time for, and additional explanations that you might need are all things that you can keep in reserve.

5. Click on the **Submit** button. The Content Area will be added to your course. A link to the Content Area will also be added to the Course Menu:

What's next?

You can add many types of content to a Content Area. In later chapters, we will cover adding images, audio, video, files for download, discussion boards, wikis, blogs, assignments, and tests. These items will be added using the tabbed menus at the top of the Content Area:

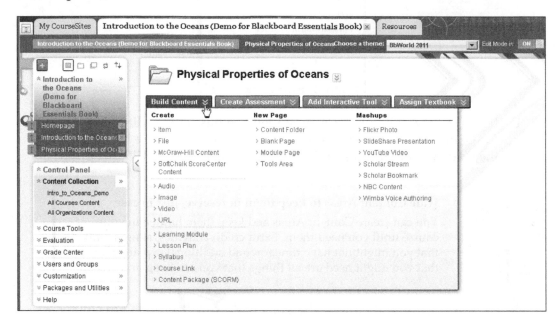

 "Adding material" is covered in Chapters 3 through 6 of this book.

Adding a Blank Page tool, which can hold any content or links that you want

The **Blank Page** tool enables you to create a Blank Page. You can add a Blank Page to your course, or to the Content Area. When you add a Blank Page to your course, a link to the page is added to the Course Menu. When you add a Blank Page to the Content Area, a link to the page is added to the Content Area.

What is a Blank Page?

In Blackboard, a Blank Page is a simple web page. You can add text, graphics, and HTML code to the page. You can also attach an item to the page.

When you want to add a page of information, and you want that information to stand by itself, a Blank Page is a good solution. Let's look at some situations where you might consider using a Blank Page.

For one of the topics, your class is taking a field trip. Under that topic's Content Area, you might add a Blank Page. On this Blank Page, you can add information about the trip, and embed a Google map.

The class has a strict code of conduct and standards, for completing work and turning it in on time. Under the main Course Menu, you might create a Blank Page of course policies. This page will always be available from the main Course Menu.

You want to create a transition from one topic to the next. Each topic is a Content Area in your course. In between the Content Areas, you can insert a Blank Page. On this page, you can put information that will help the student transition between topics.

When you create a Blank Page, consider where it will best fit into your course. If the page is as important as a topic or chapter, then add it to the Course Menu. If it's part of a topic or chapter, then add it to the Content Area for that topic.

How to add a Blank Page

Let's look at adding a Blank Page to the Course Menu, and to Content Area.

Adding a Blank Page to your course

1. In the upper-right corner of the page, ensure that **Edit Mode** is set to **ON**.

2. From the **Course Menu**, select **Create Blank Page**:

3. Blackboard will prompt you to name the Blank Page. The **Name:** field that you enter here will be displayed as a link in the Course Menu, and in a tab at the top of the course window:

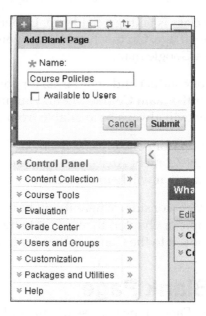

4. If you select **Available to Users**, students in this course will be able to see the Blank Page tool. If you do not make it available, it will be hidden from the students, and the link and tab for this page will not appear.

5. Click on the **Submit** button. The Blank Page tool will be added to your course:

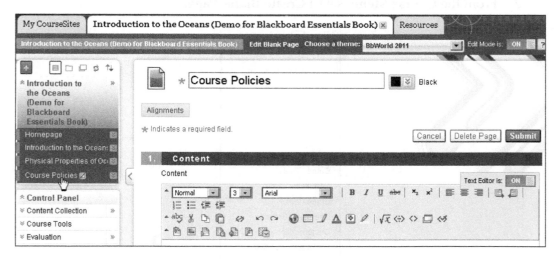

But the page is blank! Now what?

As you can see from the preceding screenshot, this really is a Blank Page. At some point, you will want to add material to the page. Keep reading for instructions.

Adding a Blank Page to the Content Area

1. In the upper-right corner of the page, ensure that **Edit Mode** is set to **ON**.

2. From the **Course Menu**, select the Content Area to which you want to add the Blank Page:

3. At the top of the Content Area, select the **Build Content** tab:

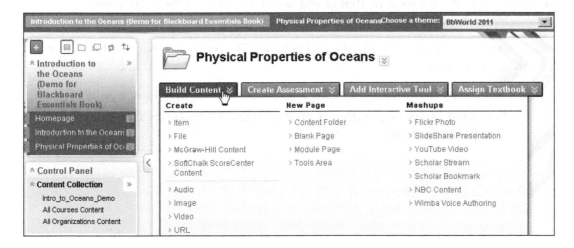

4. Under the **New Page** menu, select **Create Blank Page**.

5. Blackboard will prompt you to name the Blank Page. The name that you enter here will be displayed as a link in the Content Area.

6. If you select **Available to Users**, students on this course will be able to see the Blank Page. If you do not make it available, it will be hidden from the students, and the link for this Blank Page will not appear.

7. Click on the **Submit** button. The Blank Page will be added to your Content Area.

 But the page is blank! Now what?

As you can see from the preceding screenshot, this really is a Blank Page. At some point, you will want to add material to the page. Keep reading for instructions.

What's next?

After adding a Blank Page, you can add text, graphics, and media to that page, just like you can to any other web page. Blackboard gives you a user-friendly editor that you can use to compose the page. It is the subject of the next section.

Composing a page with the HTML editor

After you have added a Blank Page, you can use Blackboard's HTML editor to compose that page. We won't cover every function of the editor. Instead, we will cover just those functions that might not be obvious, or those that are especially useful.

Blackboard's web page editor looks and behaves like most web-based editors that you might have used:

1. In the upper-right corner of the page, ensure that **Edit Mode** is set to **ON**.

2. Select the Blank Page, either from the Course Menu or the Content Area that holds the page.

3. In the **Content** section, use the editor to write your text, as you would with any basic word processor:

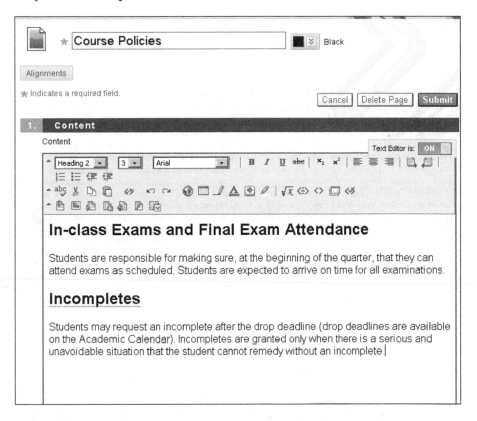

4. To insert multimedia into the page, use the Insert icons. Move the mouse pointer over each icon to see what kind of multimedia it applies to:

5. To insert HTML code into the page, such as the code that you would copy from YouTube, click on the HTML button:

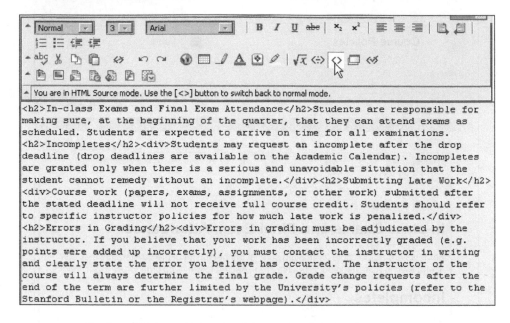

When you finish adding the HTML code, you can click on the HTML button again to return to the normal editing mode.

6. In the **Attachments** section, you can attach a file to this page. Note that you are attaching, not embedding the file.

7. In the **Options** section, you can make this page available or unavailable. You can also set the time for this page to display.

8. Clicking on the **Submit** button saves the page.

What's next?

Your Blank Page is no longer blank. It is now a page full of content in your course. But remember, in online learning, you can almost always change the content when you need it. It's your page. Update it as you wish.

Creating a sequential path for the student to work through, using a Learning Module

A Learning Module must be added to a Content Area. Similar to a Content Area, it can hold many kinds of content—static material such as web pages, links, and media; active material such as tests; and social material such as wikis and forums.

You can think of a Learning Module as a Content Area inside a Content Area.

A Learning Module can require the student to complete its material in a sequential order. This is one of the features that we will see in this section.

When to use a learning path

If you have a Content Area that has a lot of material, you can use Learning Modules to organize the Content Area into smaller sections. For example, in our course about the world's oceans, we could have a Content Area for *The Five Oceans*. Then, within that Content Area, we could create a Learning Module for each of the five oceans.

If your course is very long, consider using Learning Modules to organize the course. Also, use a Learning Module when you need to enforce a sequence in the course.

How to add a learning path

We will demonstrate how to add a Learning Module to the Content Area called *Introduction to the Oceans*.

Adding a Learning Module to a Content Area

1. In the upper-right corner of the page, ensure that **Edit Mode** is set to **ON**.
2. From the **Course Menu**, select the Content Area to which you want to add the Blank Page.
3. At the top of the Content Area, select the **Build Content** tab.

4. Under the **Create** menu, select **Learning Module**:

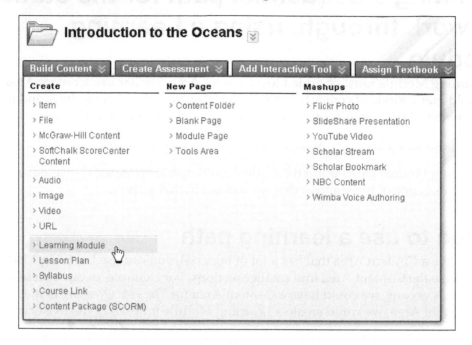

5. The **Create Learning Module** page is displayed. This page has five sections:
    ° Learning Module Information
    ° Availability
    ° View
    ° Table of Contents
    ° Submit

    Let's look at each of these sections.

6. In the **Learning Module Information** section, enter the **Name** field for the module, and also a description. In the **Availability** section, you can determine if the user can see the module yet. You can hide it, show it, or set a date for it to be visible:

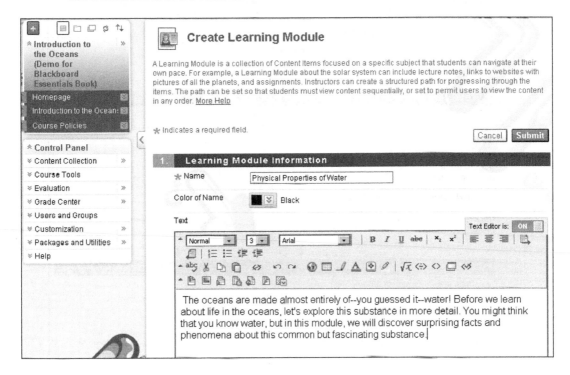

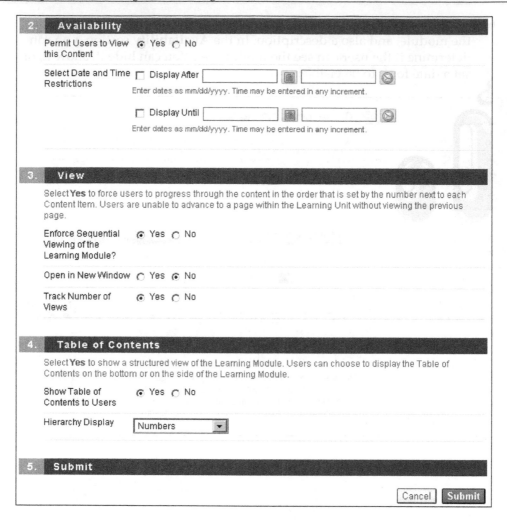

7. In the **View** section, you can force the student to view the items in the module in order. This setting does not force the user to view the items for a specific amount of time. So, the student could view a large document or video for only one second, and then immediately move on to the next item. You require students to view the items in order, but you cannot force them to read or pay attention to the items.

8. Also in the **View** section, you can make the module open in a new window, and track the number of times the module was opened. Note that these settings affect the module, not the items in the module. So when a student clicks on the name of the module, the module launches in a new window. But the items in that module do not open new windows unless you indicate that for each item.

9. The **Table of Contents** section enables you to automatically create a table of contents for the items in the module. In the following screenshot, notice the table of contents on the left-hand side. Also, notice that each item in the module is numbered:

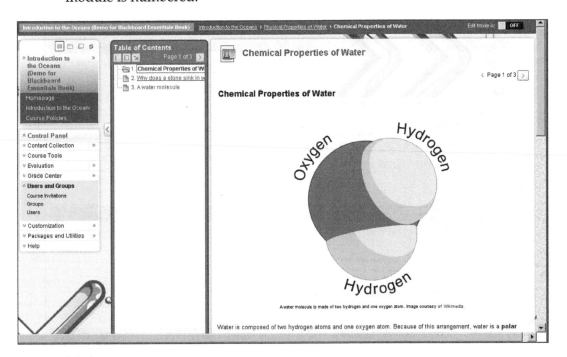

What you see in the preceding screenshot, is the result of the settings shown in the following screenshot:

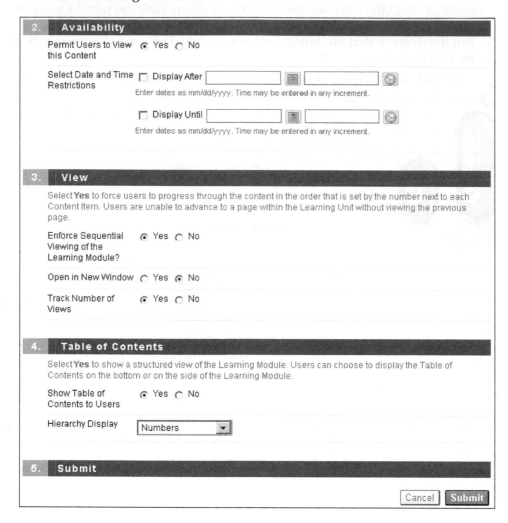

10. Finally, the **Submit** button saves your work and adds the Learning Module to the Content Area.

What's next?

You can add many types of content to a Learning Module. In later chapters, we will cover adding images, audio, video, files for download, discussion boards, wikis, blogs, assignments, and tests. These items will be added using the tabbed menus at the top of the screen, in the Learning Area:

Adding material is covered in Chapters 3 through 6, of this book.

About the Availability and View settings

Throughout this chapter, when adding items to a course, you have seen settings for **Availability** and **View**:

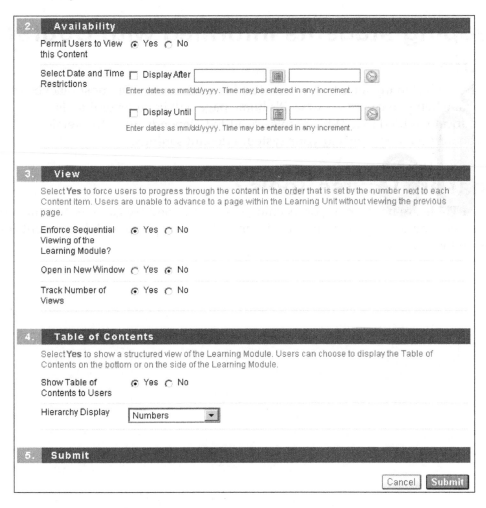

For almost all items that you add to a course, you will see these settings.

Permit Users to View this Content determines if students can see the item. Teachers can always see the item.

Select Date and Time Restrictions makes the item visible to the students only during the time that you enter. If you are going to reuse this course, you will need to edit this time period every time you run the course again. Consider creating a Blank Page, with its **Availability** set to **No**. Only teachers will be able to see that Blank Page. Then, add reminders to the page about things the teacher must do when copying and reusing the course.

Keeping students informed with Course Tools

Blackboard has many tools that you can add to your course. On most Blackboard systems, when you create a course, it's home page will have several tools automatically added to it. Which tools are added, depends upon the version of Blackboard you are using and your system's default settings.

What are Course Tools?

Course Tools are not learning or teaching materials. They are gadgets and functions that enable you to keep your students informed, and help you and the students to manage the course:

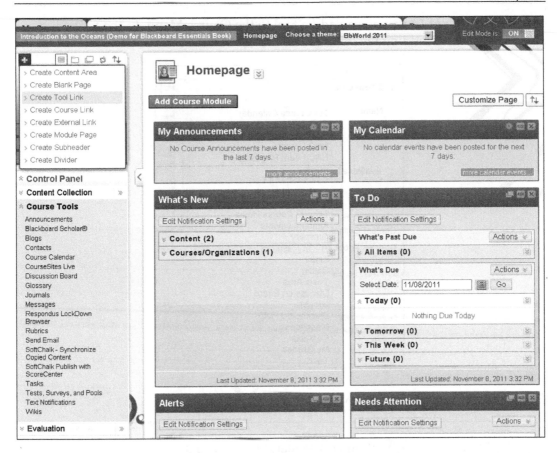

Notice in the preceding screenshot, that our demonstration course's **Homepage**
has the tools **My Announcements**, **My Calendar**, **What's New**, **To Do**, **Alerts**, and
Needs Attention. There are other tools that can be added to the course. Also, notice
that the user has selected **Create Tool Link** from the Course Menu. This is how we
add new tools to a course.

Using **Create Tool Link**, you can add a tool to the Course Menu. In the following screenshot, we are adding the link:

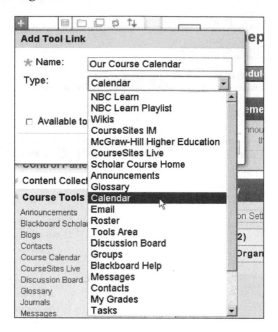

The result is shown in the following screenshot:

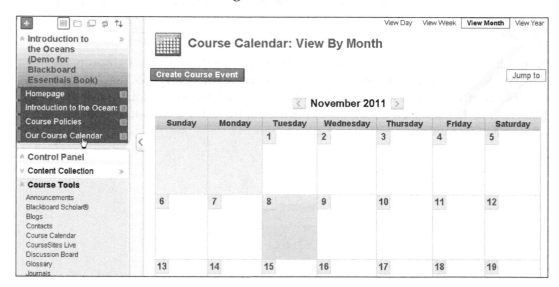

This is the same course calendar that is on the course's home page. Why would we give it a link in the Course Menu instead of just putting it on the home page? There are two reasons: first, if the tool is especially important, you might want to have it at both the home page and the Course Menu; second, if the tool requires a full screen to see all the information, you might want to give the tool its own link so that it opens in its own page. In the screenshot of the home page a few pages earlier, look at how much room **My Calendar** has, against the amount of room it has in the immediate preceding screenshot.

How to add Course Tools

Let's look at how to add Course Tools to both the Course Menu and the home page.

Adding a Course Tool to the Course Menu

1. In the upper-right corner of the page, ensure that **Edit Mode** is set to **ON**.

2. From the **Add Menu Item** list, select **Create Tool Link**.

3. Select the tool that you want to add:

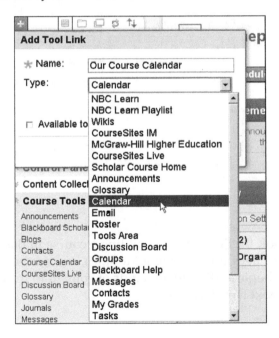

4. Enter **Name:** for the tool.

5. Set the tool's **Availability** by clicking on the checkbox next to **Available to Users**.

6. Click on the **Submit** button. A link for the tool is added to the Course Menu.

Adding a Course Tool to the home page

1. Select the course's home page.

2. In the upper-right corner of the page, ensure that **Edit Mode** is set to **ON**.

3. Click on the **Add Course Module** button. The system will display a list of modules and tools that you can add.

4. Next to the tool that you want to add, click on the **Add** button. The tool will be added to the home page.

5. To move the tools around the home page, click on the reposition button in the upper-right corner:

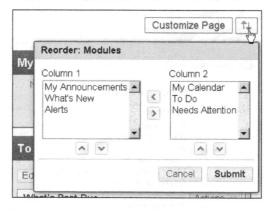

Summary

In this chapter, we took the first steps to building a course in Blackboard. By adding Content Areas, Blank Pages, and Learning Modules, we created a structure for our course. Now, we can begin adding many kinds of content to the course. That will be the subject of the next few chapters.

3

Adding Static Material to a Course

In the previous chapter, you learned how to add Content Areas and Learning Modules. These were blank areas, ready to be filled with course content. In this chapter, you will learn how to add static course material. **Static course material** is course content that the student reads, views, or listens to, but does not interact with.

In addition to learning how to upload your own files, you will also learn how to use files in Content Collection, which other people in your organization have uploaded.

In this chapter, you will be learning how to do the following:

- Adding a file for students to download
- Adding a video to your course
- Accessing files in Content Collection, which other users in your system have uploaded
- Uploading files in Content Collection so that other users in your system can access the files
- Adding a web link to your course
- Adding an image to your course

Adding a file for students to download

There are two ways to add a file for students to download. You can add the file as a file, or add it as an item. We'll look at both options.

File versus item

In the following screenshot, we have added two documents to the course. They are the first and second things on the page, **Water Inventory Homework.rtf** and **Ocean Salinity**. They are both .rtf or word-processing documents. The first one was added as a file, and the second as an item:

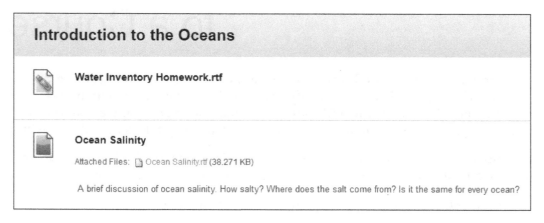

Notice that **Water Inventory Homework.rtf**, the one added as a file, consists of only a title. This title is the link to the file. When clicked, the link will download or open the file. Notice that **Ocean Salinity**, the one added as an item, consists of a title, a description, and a link to the file. In both cases, you are supplying a file to your students.

If the file requires explanation, consider adding it as an item. If the title will give your students enough information about the file, consider adding it as a file.

Content Collections

When a file is added to a course, that file will also be added to the **Course Content** area:

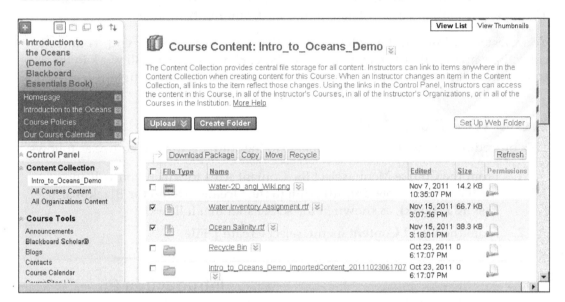

Notice that in the preceding screenshot, the **Course Content** area for **Intro_to_ Oceans_Demo_ImportedContent_20111023061707** is part of the user's **Content Collection**. The Content Collection is available to the teacher and the creator of the course. Teachers can create links to the content in the collection. So you can add a file once, and link to it many times. By default, the Content Collection is not available to students. Teachers make a specific piece of content available to the students by linking to that piece of content from the course.

Not all Blackboard installations have access to the Content Collection system. If your school does not subscribe to this piece of the Blackboard system, you will see "Files" instead of "Content Collection", and see the Content Collection for just one course at a time.

In the preceding screenshot, notice that there are three Content Collection areas. The first one is a list of files added to the course. The second is a list of files added to all of the courses that this teacher can access. The third Content Collection area, **All Organizations Content**, links to content that is provided by organizations. This is shown only if your installation has the Community system.

Your System Administrator will set up the Content Collections for you. Your content collections might differ from what you see here. However, they will work in the same way—as a repository for sharing and reusing files among courses.

How to add a file

This procedure will make the file available to the students in your course as follows:

1. From the Course Menu, select the Content Area to which you will add the file, for example, **Introduction to the Oceans (Demo for Blackboard Essential Book)**, as shown in the screenshot that follows.

2. From the **Build Content** menu, select **Create | File**:

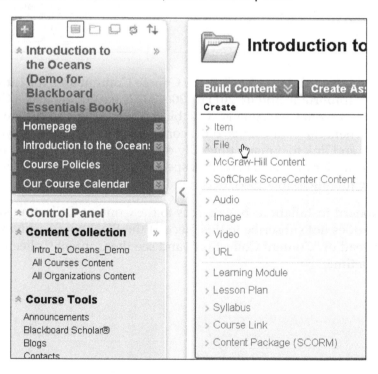

3. The **Create File** page is displayed:

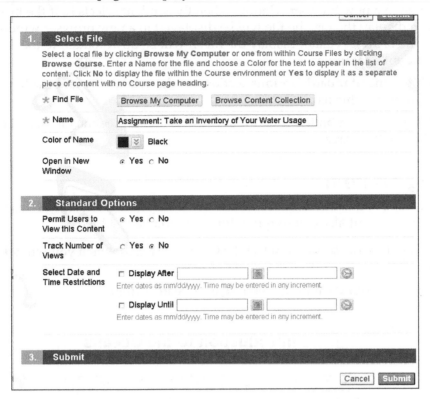

4. Under the **Find File** section, you can use the **Browse My Computer** button to select a file that is on your computer, or on a drive connected to your computer. You can also use the **Browse Content Collection** button to select a file that is in one of your **Content Collection** areas.

5. The **Name** field that you enter will be displayed on the page to which you are adding this file.

6. Under the **Open in New Window** section, if you select **Yes**, the file will open in a new browser window when the student selects it. If the browser can display the file, the file will be displayed in a new browser window. If the browser cannot display the file, it will be downloaded to the student's computer.

7. Under the **Standard Options** section, set the availability and tracking options for this file.

8. Click on the **Submit** button to save it. You should see the file added to the Content Area.

Adding an item

In this section, we'll show you how to add an item, so that the student can see not only the title, but also a description for what you have added:

1. From the Course Menu, select the Content Area to which you will add the item.

2. From the **Build Content** menu, select **Create | Item**:

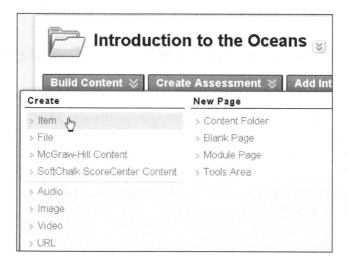

3. The **Edit Item** page is displayed:

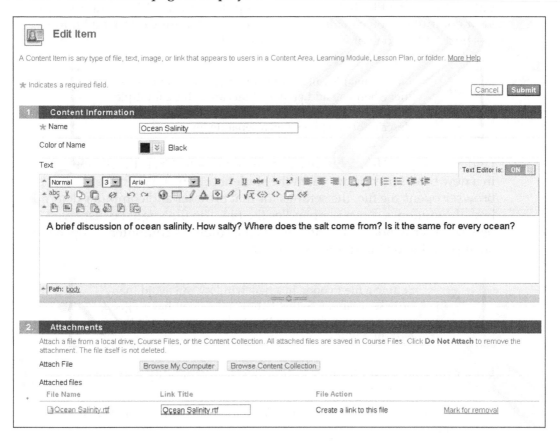

4. The **Name** that you enter will be displayed on the page to which you are adding this file.

5. The description that you enter into the text editor will also be displayed on the page. Notice that this is a full-featured text editor. You can add anything to the description that you put on a web page.

> When entering the description for the item, remember that there might be other things in the same Content Area. If you add a long description, the page for the Content Area can get very long.

6. Under the **Attachments** section, you can use the **Browse My Computer** button to select a file that is on your computer, or on a drive connected to your computer. You can also use the **Browse Content Collection** button to select a file in one of your Content Collection areas.

Notice that it's called **Attachments**. Unlike adding a file, when you add an item, you can include multiple files. Also, attachments appear under the filename and description, displayed on a separate line.

7. Under the **Open New Window** section, if you select **Yes**, the file will open in a new browser window when the student selects it. When the student's browser opens the file, the settings for that browser and computer determine how the student's computer handles the file. The file might be displayed in a new browser window, downloaded to the student's computer, or opened by an application on the student's computer.

Setting a file to open in a new window can avoid many browser issues. Use this setting unless you have a good reason to open the file in the student's browser in the current window.

8. Under the **Standard Options** section, set the availability and tracking options for this item.

9. Click on the **Submit** button to save. You should see the item added to the Content Area.

What's next?

Now that the file is added to your course, it also appears in the Content Area. You can add multiple links to the file. If your System Administrator has allowed sharing between courses, other teachers can add the file to their course.

Adding a video to your course

There are several ways to add multimedia to your course. You can upload the file directly to Blackboard, just like you did with a file in the previous section, or you can link to the media on another site, such as YouTube or Vimeo. Finally, you can embed the video on a page in your course. The following table compares the methods available to you:

Uploading a file	Linking to a video-sharing site	Embedding a video on a Blank Page in your course
For example, uploading .mpg, .wav, .wmv, .mov, and so on directly onto Blackboard.	For example, linking to media on www.youtube.com or www.vimeo.com.	For example, embedding a YouTube video in a web page.
Blackboard embeds the video in the Content Area, and displays it on the page with the rest of the content.	Blackboard shows the link to the video site.	Blackboard shows the link to the page.
The student's browser plays the video.	When students click on the link, they are taken to the video site. The video site takes care of playing the video.	When students click on the link, they are taken to the page in the course. The video site's player is embedded on the page, so the video site takes care of playing the video.
Keeps all the content on one page. However, the Content Area page can get long.	Puts a link on your Content Area page, so it doesn't take much room. However, the student is taken to a different site for the video and you might not have control over that site.	Puts a link on your Content Area page, so it does not take much room and you can add text to the page where the video is embedded, to explain the video. However, the video is still being hosted on someone else's site, where you don't have full control over it.

The first method in the preceding table, uploading a video to your course, has some disadvantages. Blackboard is not a streaming video server. If your video is large in file size, or many students try to access it at once, your Blackboard server can slow down (or even fail) under the load. However, uploading the video to your own Blackboard installation ensures that you have control over it. You might even be forbidden from putting the video on a sharing site, because of confidentiality issues.

When you put the video on an external site such as YouTube or Vimeo, unless you register for a premium account on either site, your video will be available to the public. This might be unacceptable to your institution. However, these sites are optimized for delivering videos. You won't need to worry about performance issues if several students try to play the video at the same time.

Let's look at each method.

Uploading a video in your course

When you have the video on your computer, instead of on another website, you can upload the video in Blackboard and serve it directly to your students:

1. From the Course Menu, select the Content Area to which you will add the file.

2. From the **Build Content** menu, select **Create | Video**.

3. The **Create Video** page is displayed.

4. Under the **Find File** section, you can use the **Browse My Computer** button to select a file that is on your computer, or on a drive connected to your computer. You can also use the **Browse Content Collection** button to select a file that is in one of your Content Collection areas.

> When searching for videos and other material to add to your course, consider starting your search at www.creativecommons.org.

5. The **Name** field that you enter will be displayed on the page to which you are adding this video.

6. Under the **Dimensions** section if you resize the video, it will be displayed at the new size. You might distort the video if you choose different proportions.

7. Under **Standard Options**, set the availability and tracking options for this video.

8. Click on the **Submit** button to save it. You should see the video added to the Content Area:

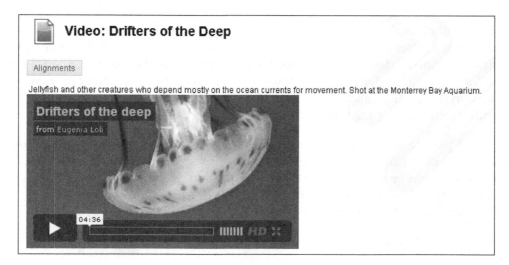

Linking to a video that is on another site

Instead of embedding the video on a page in your course, you might want to send the student out to the video-hosting site. And, it is certainly faster to just create a link than it is to create a page:

1. From the Course Menu, select the Content Area to which you will add the file.

2. From the **Build Content** menu, select **Create | URL**.

3. The **Create URL** page is displayed.

4. The **Name** that you enter will be displayed on the page to which you are adding this link.

5. The **URL** is the link itself. The URL will not be displayed.

6. The description that you enter in the text editor will also be displayed on the page. Notice that this is a full-featured text editor. You can add anything to the description that you can put on a web page.

[When entering the description for the item, remember that there might be other things in the same Content Area. If you add a long description, the page for the Content Area can get very long.]

7. You can add an **Attachment** field; it will get its own link, next to the one for the website that you entered in the **URL** field.

8. If you select **Open in New Window**, the link will open in a new browser window or tab. This new window will show only the video site. If you do not select this option, the page that is being linked to it will appear in the same window. However, the **Course Menu** field and other items in the sidebars will not be displayed while the page is being viewed. There will be a Blackboard navigation menu across the top of the page. The rest of the page will belong to the video-sharing site.

The following screenshot shows the result when you select **Open in New Window**:

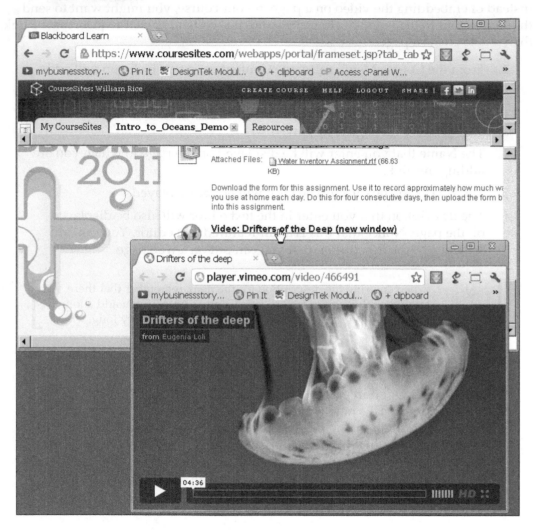

9. It looks similar to the following screenshot, when you do not select **Open in New Window**:

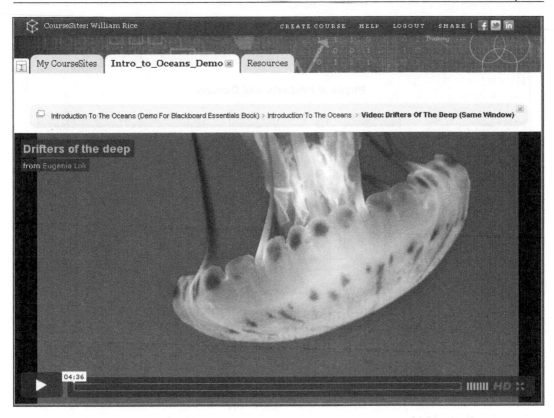

10. Click on the **Submit** button to save it. You should see the link, its description, and any attachments, added to the Content Area.

Embedding a video on a Blank Page

This will keep your students on your course site, even though the video itself is hosted on the external site. Embedding the video on a page enables you to add your own explanatory text around the video. This makes the video a seamless part of the page:

1. From the **Course Menu** field, select the Content Area to which you want to add the Blank Page.

2. At the top of the Content Area section, select the **Build Content** tab:

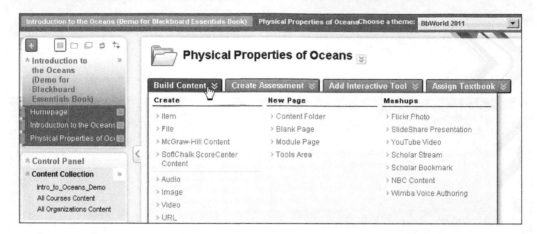

3. Under the **New Page** menu, select **Blank Page**.

4. Blackboard will prompt you to name the Blank Page. The **Name** field that you enter here will be displayed as a link in the Content Area.

5. If you select **Available to Users**, students in this course will be able to see the Blank Page. If you do not make it available, it will be hidden from students, and the link for this Blank Page will not appear.

6. Click on the **Submit** button. The Blank Page will be added to your Content Area.

7. In the **Content** section, use the editor to write your text as you would with any basic word processor:

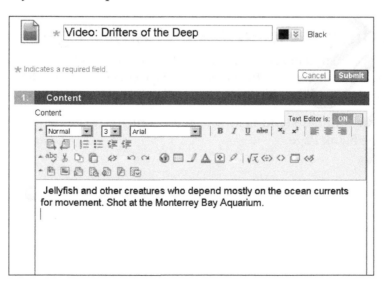

Embedding a video that is hosted on another site

To embed a video that is hosted on another site, such as www.youtube.com or www.vimeo.com, you will need to use an HTML code as follows:

1. In your browser, launch another window. Keep the page in Blackboard open in the background.

2. Go to the site that is hosting the video. In this example, we are using player.vimeo.com/video/466491:

3. On the video's page, you should see some HTML code that you can copy. For example, on Vimeo, there will be a button labeled **EMBED** that you can click, to reveal the HTML code:

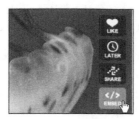

On YouTube, there will be a button labeled **SHARE**, which opens a new panel. Then you will click on the **EMBED** link, which reveals the HTML code.

4. Copy the HTML code:

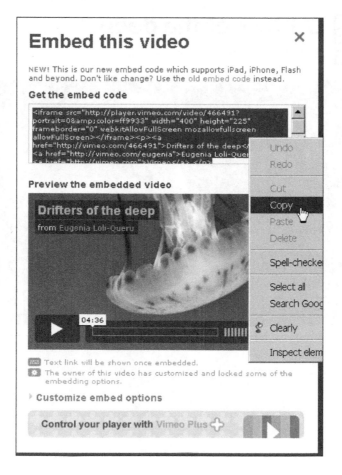

5. Switch back to your course in Blackboard.

6. In the page editor, click on the HTML button:

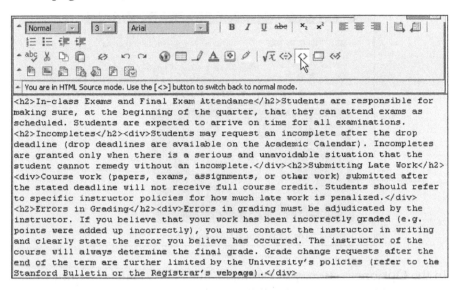

7. Paste the code that you copied from the video site:

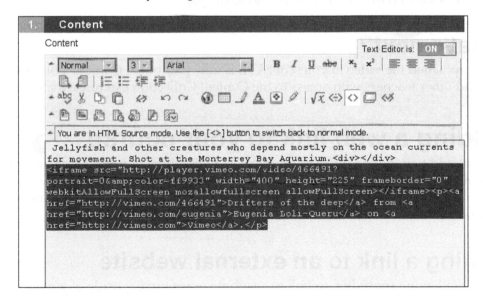

8. Click on the HTML button again to switch back to normal view. You should see the video embedded on the page:

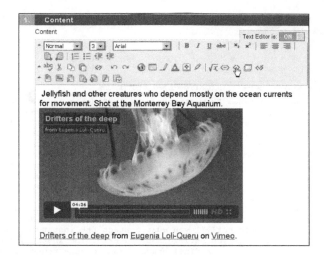

9. In the **Options** section, you can make this page available or unavailable. You can also set the time for this page to display.

10. Clicking on the **Submit** button saves the page.

What's next?

If you uploaded the video in your course, it is now part of the Content Collection. You and other teachers with access to the Content Collection can reuse the video.

Adding a web link to your course

You can add two types of links to a course. As with other Learning Management Systems, you can add links to websites. Blackboard also offers a fast and easy way to add links to other material in your course. This makes it easy to reuse content from your course.

Adding a link to an external website

Use the following procedure to link to a website or resource outside of your Blackboard course:

1. From the Course Menu, select the Content Area to which you will add the file.

2. From the **Build Content** menu, select **Create | URL**.

3. The **Create URL** page is displayed.

4. The **Name:** field that you enter will be displayed on the page to which you are adding this link.

5. The **URL** is the link itself. It will not be displayed.

6. The **Description** field that you enter in text editor will also be displayed on the page. Notice that this is a full-featured text editor. You can add anything to the description that you put on a web page.

7. You can add an **Attachment** field; it will get its own link next to the one for the website that you entered in the **URL** field.

8. If you select **Open in New Window**, the link will open in a new browser window or tab. This new window will show only the external site. If you do not select this option, the page that is being linked to will appear in the same window. However, the Course Menu and other items in the sidebars will not be displayed while the page is being viewed. There will be a Blackboard navigation menu across the top of the page. The rest of the page will belong to the external site, as shown in the following screenshot:

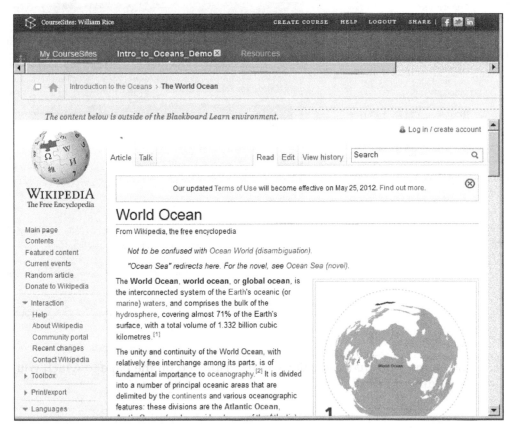

9. Click on the **Submit** button to save it. You should see the link, its description, and any attachments, added to the Content Area.

Adding a link to a Course Asset

Before you begin this procedure, you must have some content in your course to link to, for example, a file, Content Area page, link, or activity. You can't link to something in a blank course, because there's nothing to link to:

1. From the Course Menu, select the Content Area to which you will add the file.

2. From the **Build Content** menu, select **Create | Course Link**.

3. The **Course Link Information** page is displayed.

4. Click on the **Browse...** button. A pop-up window is displayed, listing all of the assets in the course:

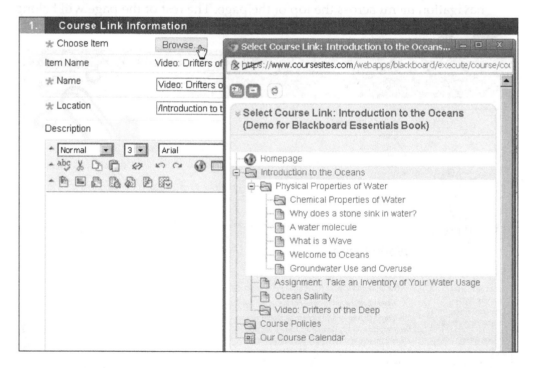

5. Click on the item to select it.

6. The **Name** field that you enter will be displayed on the page to which you are adding this link.

7. The **Location** field is filled in for you. You can edit this field, but it will break the link. Therefore, do not edit the location!

8. The description that you enter in the text editor will also be displayed on the page.

9. Unlike when you link to an external website, there is no option to attach a file or to open the link in a new window.

10. Select **Standard Options** for this link.

11. Click on the **Submit** button to save it. You should see the link and its description, added to the Content Area.

The links for **external websites** and **internal course links** have slightly different icons:

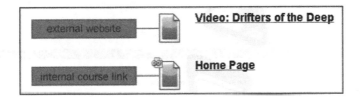

Blackboard supports several sets of icons. The ones used by your installation might be different than the ones shown here.

Adding an image to your course

There are several ways to add an image to your course. You can create a new Blank Page and add the image to that. Essentially, you are giving the image its own page. If you do this, a link to the page will appear in the Content Area to which you added the page. You can keep the name of the link and its description short. This enables you to add an image to a Content Area without taking up much room on the Content Area page.

Also, you can add an image directly to a Content Area. If you do this, the image will appear on the Content Area. It will take up more room than a link to another page, but your students won't need to click on a link to see the image.

We have already covered how to add a Blank Page, earlier in this chapter. In the following procedure, we will cover how to add an image directly to a Content Area.

Adding an image to a Content Area

1. From the Course Menu, select the Content Area to which you will add the image.

2. From the **Build Content** menu, select **Create | Image**.

3. The **Create Image** page is displayed:

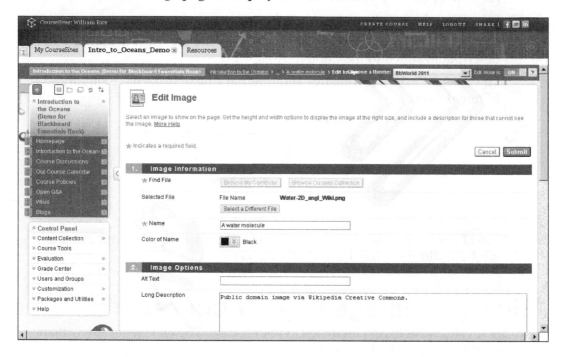

4. Under the **Find File** section, you can use the **Browse My Computer** button to select an image that is on your computer, or on a drive connected to your computer. You can also use the **Browse Content Collection** button to select an image that is present in one of your Content Collection areas.

5. The **Name** field that you enter will be displayed on the page to which you are adding this image.

6. The **Alt Text** field is displayed when the user points to the image, and is also used to help visually-impaired users to navigate the page.

7. The **Long Description** field is displayed on the page along with the image.

8. Under **Dimensions**, if you resize the image it will be displayed at the new size. You might distort the image if you choose different proportions.

9. If the image is too big to display on the same page as the rest of the items in the Content Area, consider setting **Open Target in New Window** to **Yes**.

10. Under **Standard Options**, set the availability and tracking options for this image.

11. Click on the **Submit** button to save it. You should see the image added to the Content Area.

Summary

In this chapter, we saw how to add several kinds of static content to a course. We used links and embedding to include the content in our course. Blackboard also has special functions for adding other kinds of static content, such as photos from www.flickr.com, textbooks from *McGraw-Hill*, videos and other assets from NBC, and so on. Using the methods learnt in this chapter, you'll be able to add these other content types.

4
Discussion Boards

In the previous chapter, you learned how to add static material to a course. In this chapter, we will discuss how to add interaction to a course using Discussion Board. The activities that we will cover enable students to collaborate with each other and with the instructor. These activities require feedback and guidance from the instructor to make them work. In this chapter, we will cover the following:

- Creating forums with Discussion Board
- Creating links to specific forums
- Collecting posts in a forum
- Grading posts in a forum

About Discussion Boards

Your course's Discussion Board enables students to interact with each other, and also with the instructor. Discussions can be as follows:

- Moderated or unmoderated
- Graded or ungraded
- Attributed or anonymous

Depending upon your installation, there could be a default Discussion Board for each course. The Discussion Board consists of one or more forums. Each forum contains threads. So the hierarchy is as follows:

- Discussion Board (there is one default created for your course)
- Forum (there can be many)
- Thread (there can be many)

The following screenshot shows our course's Discussion Board with two forums:

Let's begin by learning to use the course's default Discussion Board.

Creating forums with Discussion Board

By itself, the default Discussion Board is of no use. To give students a place to hold discussions, you must create at least one forum.

To create a forum, perform the following steps:

1. Select **Course Tools | Discussion Board**.

2. The page displays all of the Discussion Boards in the course. In our example course, there is only one board so far, that is, the default board for the course named **Intro to the Oceans (Demo for Blackboard Essentials Book)**:

3. Select the default **Discussion Board**. In this example, we click on **Intro to Oceans Demo**. The **Discussion Board** is displayed. Remember that you are looking at this from the instructor's point of view. Students cannot create a new forum.

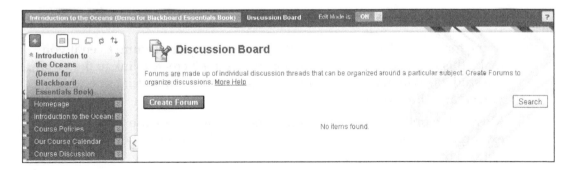

4. Click on the **Create Forum** button. The **Create Forum** page is displayed.

5. In the forum-information area, enter **Name** and **Description** for the forum. Students will see these when the forum is listed on the Discussion Board:

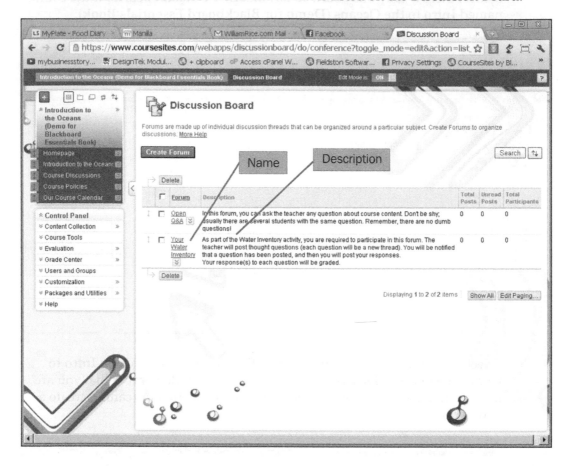

6. In the forum-availability area, set the availability of the forum. Even if you make this forum available to students, if you don't create a link to the forum, the students will never see it. For now, make the forum available, and we will create a link to it later.

7. Most of the options under the **Forum Settings** area are self-explanatory. For example, you can make the forum posts graded. However, here are some options that we will explain:

    °   When a user subscribes to the forum, the user will receive an e-mail notifying him or her of new posts to the forum. The instructor can determine how the e-mail is generated. You can either send a link to the Discussion Board or send full text of the posting within the e-mail.

○ If you select **Allow Members to Rate Posts**, then each student will be able to rate posts made by other students. They won't be able to rate posts made by the instructor. The standard scale for rating posts is one to five stars. In the following screenshot, a student named Suzy is rating a post made by another student named Sammy:

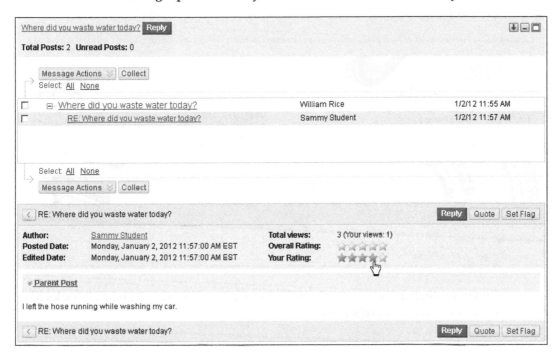

Allowing students to rate each other's posts enables you to see the amount of consensus that the class has about a post:

○ If you select **Force Moderation of Posts**, then each time a student posts, the moderator must review the post. The moderator can publish or deny the post. By default, the instructor is the moderator. However, using the forums' **Manage** option, you can make any student a moderator.

8. From the students' view, the following screenshot shows what it looks like when the student is waiting for his or her post to be moderated:

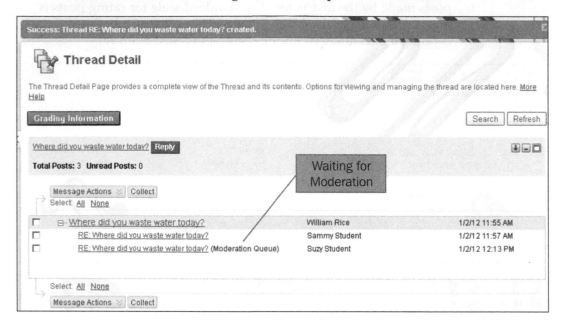

From the instructor's view, the following screenshot shows what it looks like to moderate a student's post:

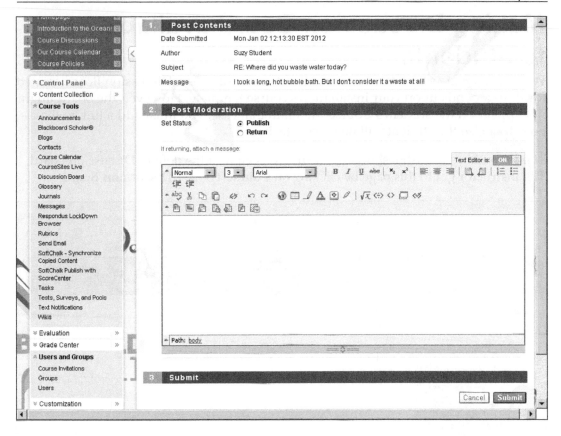

- ° Under **Forum Settings**, in the **Grade** section, you can choose to give the student a grade for the entire forum, or for each thread in the forum.

9. To save your work and create the forum, click on the **Submit** button.

In a later section, you will see how to create a link to this forum.

Making Discussion Board available to students

When you create a course, sometimes it automatically has a Discussion Board created for it. It depends upon your installation's course template. However, the board might not appear on the student's Course Menu. In that case, you must add a link to the board, or else the student will never see the board.

The following screenshot shows the instructor's view of the default Discussion Board. The instructor got to this page by clicking on **Course Tools | Discussion Board**:

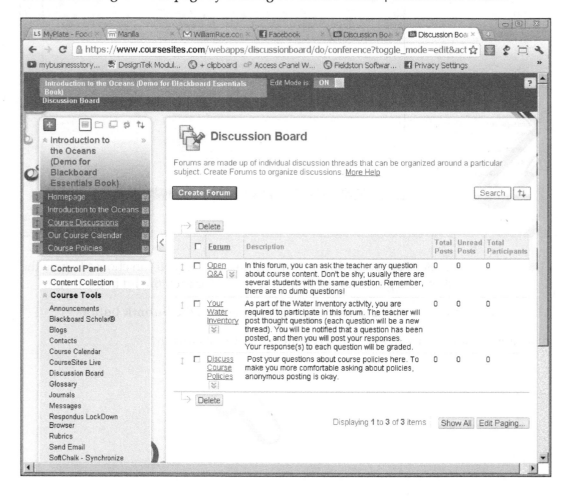

In this example, the student doesn't have a Discussion Board link. You must create a link to the board, or link to the individual forums on the board.

Adding a link to Discussion Board on the Course Menu

If you give students a link to Discussion Board, they will see a list of all of the forums in the course. You can also give them links to one forum at a time.

To create a link to **Discussion Board on Course Menu**, perform the following steps:

1. From the **Add Menu Item** menu, select **Create Tool Link**:

2. The **Create Tool Link** dialog box is displayed. In the **Name** field, enter the name for the link. Students will see this in the Course Menu.
3. From the **Type** drop-down list, select **Discussion Board**.
4. Mark it as **Available to Users**.
5. To save the link, click on the **Submit** button.

Remember that while the link you create will display whatever name you enter, the Discussion Board page will always have the title **Discussion Board** displayed at the top:

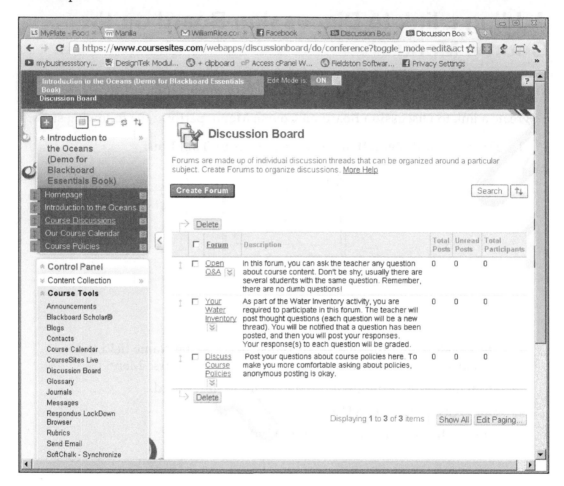

Creating a link to a forum

You can link directly to a forum. When the student clicks on the link, he or she is taken to the forum. Note that the thread crumbs at the top of the page show the Discussion Board is one level up from the forum:

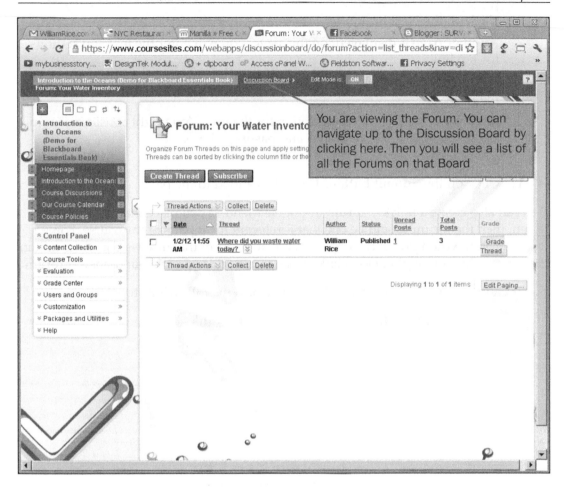

To add a link to a forum on Content Area, perform the following steps:

1. From **Course Menu**, select the **Content Area** to which you will add the link.

2. From the **Build Content** menu, select **Add Interactive Tool | Discussion Board**.

3. The **Create Link to Discussion Board** page is displayed. On this page, you will select the forum to link to.

4. Select the **radio** button for **Select a Discussion Board Forum**.

5. Select a forum to link to.

6. Click on the **Next** button.

7. Another page is displayed; on this page, you will enter the text and settings for the link.

8. In the **Link Name** field, enter the name for the link. This will be displayed to the user.

9. In the **Text** field, enter a description for the link. You might consider copying the description from the forum and pasting it here.

10. Set **Availability** of the link.

11. Click on the **Submit** button. The link is added to the page.

You can also create a link to a forum in Course Menu. If you place the link in Course Menu, then the forum should be one that is relevant to all parts of the course. For example, you would probably not place a link to a forum that discusses just one unit in the course. But you might place a link to the course-wide, question-and-answer forum.

To add a link to a forum in Course Menu, perform the following steps:

1. From **Add Menu Item**, select **Create Course Link**:

2. The **Add Course Link** dialog box is displayed. In the **Name** field, enter the name for the link. Students will see this in Course Menu.

3. Click on the **Browse** button. Another pop-up window is displayed, which shows all the assets in the course that you can link to:

4. Select the forum to which you will link. In our example, we will select **Open Q&A**.

5. Mark it as **Available to Users**.

6. To save the link, click on the **Submit** button.

Course links are not just for forums.

You can use this technique to link to any asset in your course. Look at the screenshot in step 3 of the preceding procedure, and you'll see that all of the Course Assets show up on the list of possible links.

Managing a forum

Now that you have created a forum and your students are posting in it, you can start managing the forum. Blackboard offers several features for this.

Collecting posts in a forum

Blackboard enables you to select individual posts in a forum, and then display just the selected posts on a single page. Let's look at a simple example.

In this forum, the instructor started a thread with a post called **Where did you waste water today?** Then, two students responded as shown in the following screenshot:

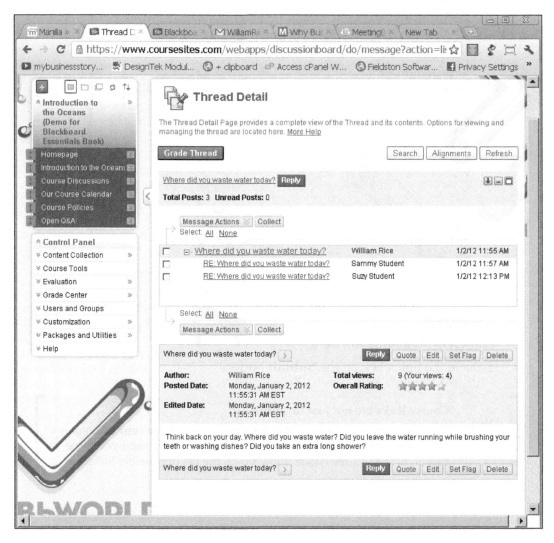

Suppose that we want to see the students' posts collected on one page. First, we select these posts by clicking on the checkbox next to them:

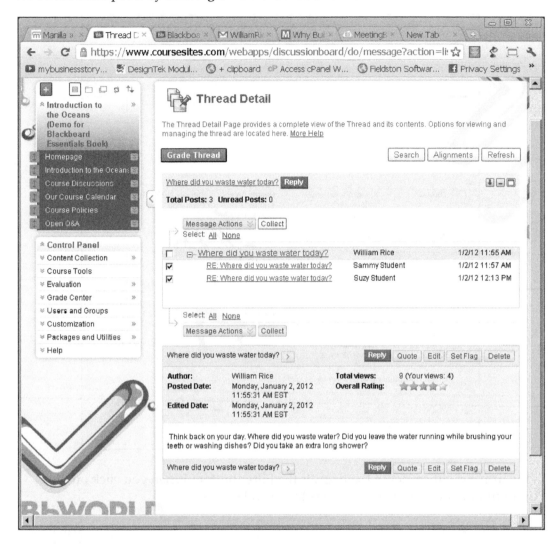

Then, we click on the **Collect** button. The result is a page containing only the selected posts; this page shows not only the subject, but also the content of the posts:

In the upper-right corner of the page, is the **Filter** button. When you click on the **Filter** button, you can search for posts by several criteria:

Once you have collected and filtered the posts, you can print them.

Saving posts as HTML or text
Blackboard does not enable you to export posts as HTML or text. However, there is a workaround. Read further to know more.

When you are viewing Forum Collection, click on the **Print Preview** button; Blackboard will open two new windows. First, it will open a window showing just the **Collection**. In the following screenshot, this is the window on the right-hand side of the screen. Then, it will open a window with a **Print** dialog box. In the following screenshot, this is the window on the left-hand side of the screen.

To save the posts as HTML, ignore the **Print** dialog box. Instead, select the window containing just the collected posts, and save it as a web page.

In most browsers, you will right-click on that window and select **Save as...** or **Save page as...**. Once you have saved the collected posts as HTML, you can use any HTML editor (or even most word processors , such as Word and OpenOffice) to edit the text.

 This procedure might differ slightly in different browsers, but viewing the Collection and saving it as a web page is common to them all. The exact clicks for saving as a web page might be slightly different.

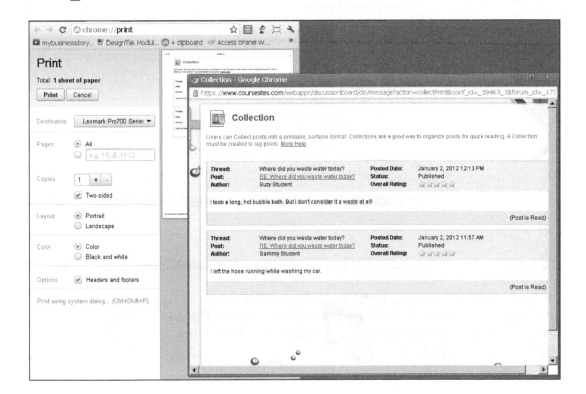

Grading posts in a forum

When you created the forum, you determined whether:

- The forum would be ungraded
- The student would receive one grade for all his/her participation in the forum
- Each thread would be graded

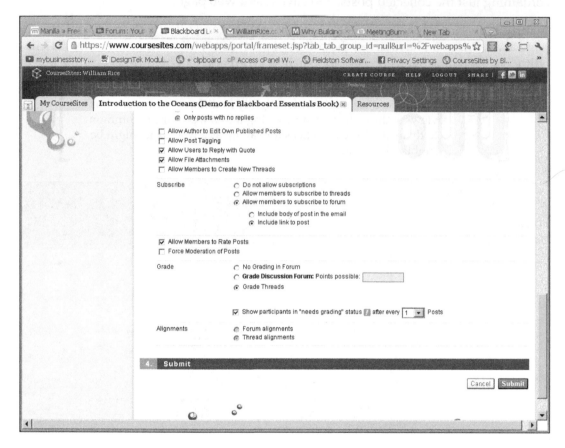

To grade a forum, navigate to the front page of that forum. If **Grade Forum** is activated, you will see a **Grade Forum** button. If **Grade Threads** is activated, you will see a **Grade Thread** button next to each thread. Click on the button to begin the grading process:

This brings you to a page that lists the individual postings in this thread. From this page, click on the **Grade** button for each posting, and then assign it a grade:

Summary

An online course can often leave students feeling isolated from their classmates, and from the instructor. Forums can help to overcome this. They provide a way to encourage discussion among the students, and can give insight into the students' attitudes and feelings about the course.

You can encourage your students to use the forums by:

- Providing convenient links to the forums
- Presenting students with thought-provoking and funny questions for discussion
- Grading students' posts

In the next chapter, we will cover blogs and wikis. We will learn about the mechanics of adding them to a course, using, and managing them. We will also discuss when they are appropriate and how to include them in the flow of a course.

5
Blogs and Wikis

In this chapter, we will cover adding blogs and wikis to a course. These activities enable students to collaborate with each other, and with the teacher. These activities usually require feedback and guidance from the teacher to make them work well.

In this chapter, you will learn how to do the following:

- Adding a blog to your course
- Adding a wiki to your course
- Understanding when to use blogs and wikis
- Monitoring and managing blogs and wikis

We'll look at the capabilities and limitations of each tool, to help you decide when to use each one. We will also see how they blend into the flow of a course.

About blogs

A **blog** provides a place for students to express their thoughts and discuss course material. In a forum, you can restrict students from creating new threads. In a blog, students have the freedom to create new entries.

Combine blogs and wikis to complete the learning cycle

In a blog, entries and comments are organized chronologically. This makes a blog a good tool for publicly documenting and discussing a journey, or continuing a project. A wiki is organized as per topic. This makes it a good tool for categorizing and organizing knowledge. While you guide the students through a journey or project, you can have them blog about their experiences. At the conclusion, you can have them assimilate and organize their knowledge into a wiki.

Individual versus class blogs

Blogs can be owned by each individual student, or by the entire class. In an individual student blog, each student is given their own blog. Only that student can post in his/her blog. In a class blog, every student can create new posts. In both cases, students can comment on posts.

Blogs Course Tool link

On **Course Menu**, you can add a **Course Tool** link called **Blogs**:

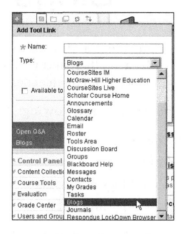

When a user clicks on this link, it displays a page that lists all of the blogs in your course:

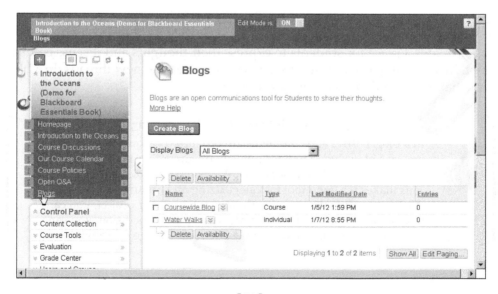

In the preceding example, **Coursewide Blog** is available only from the **Blogs** page. However, a link to the **Water Walks** blog was also added to the **Introduction to the Oceans (Demo for Blackboard Essentials Book)** page:

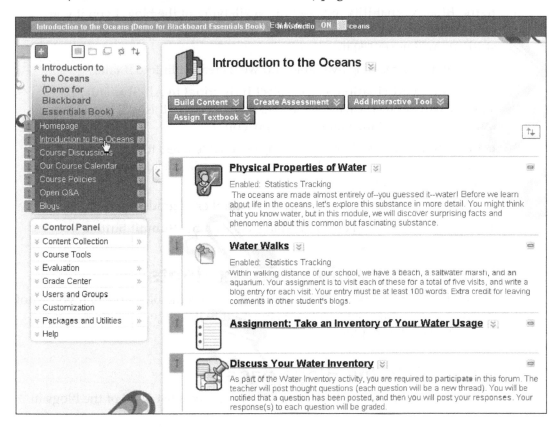

Whenever you create a blog, a link to it will always appear on the **Blogs** page. If you want a link to it on the Course Page, you will need to add it to the page.

Creating a blog

By itself, the **Blogs** page is of no use. To give students a place to blog, you must create at least one blog. To create a blog, perform the following steps:

1. Select **Course Tools | Blogs**.

2. The page displays all of the blogs in the course. If this is a new course, there are probably no blogs.

3. Click on the **Create Blog** button. The **Create Blog** page is displayed.

4. In the **Blog Information** area, enter the **Name** and **Description** fields for the blog. Students will see the name when the blog is listed on the Blogs page. They will not see the description until they click and select the blog.

5. In the **Blog Availability** area, set the availability of the blog. Even if you make this blog available to students, if you don't create a link to the blog, students will never see it.

6. For now, make the blog available and we'll create a link to it later.

7. Under **Blog Participation**, if you select **Individual to All Students**, each student will get their own blog. If you select **Course**, this will create just one blog, which all the students can post on.

8. Under **Blog Settings**, there are settings to enable users to edit and delete entries and posts. If you enable this, users can edit/delete only their own posts and comments.

9. Under **Grade Settings**, you can assign a number of grade points to the blog.

10. To save your work and create the blog, click on the **Submit** button.

Making blogs available to students

When you create a blog, a link to it will always appear on the Blogs page. If you want a link to it on a **Course** page, you will need to add it to the page. Each procedure is covered in the rest of the chapter.

Adding a link to the Blogs page

If you give students a link to the Blogs page, they will see a list of all of the blogs in the course.

To create a link to the Blogs page on **Course Menu**, perform the following steps:

1. From the **Add Menu Item** menu, select **Create Tool Link**:

2. The **Add Tool Link** dialog box is displayed. In the **Name** field, enter the name for the link. Students will see this in **Course Menu**.

3. From the **Type** drop-down list, select **Blog**.

4. Mark it as **Available to Users**.

5. To save the link, click on the **Submit** button.

Remember that while the link you create will display whatever name you enter, the **Discussion Board** page will always have the title **Blogs** displayed at the top:

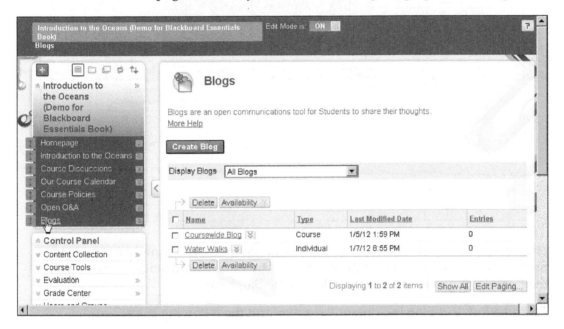

Creating a link to a blog

You can link directly to a blog. When a student clicks on the link, he/she is taken to the blog. Note that the thread crumbs at the top of the page show that the Blogs page is one level higher than this blog:

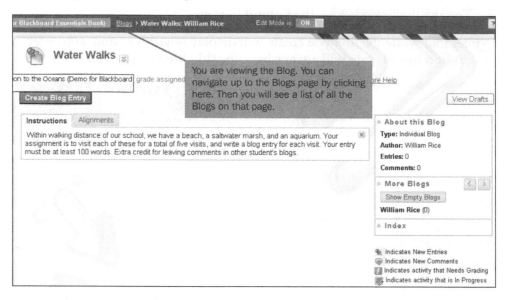

Students have a habit of exploring parts of the course that we might not be ready to reveal. So if there are blogs in the course that you don't want students to see yet, set their availability so they won't display on the Blogs page.

To add a link to a blog in Content Area, perform the following steps:

1. From **Course Menu**, select the Content Area to which you will add the link.

2. From the **Build Content** menu, select **Add Interactive Tool | Blog**.

3. The **Create Link: Blog** page is displayed.

4. Select the **radio** button for **Link to a blog**.

5. Select the blog you want to link to.

6. Click on the **Next** button.

7. Another page is displayed. On this page, you will enter the text and settings for the link.

8. In the **Link Name** field, enter the name for the link. This will be displayed to the user.

9. In the **Text** field, enter a description for the link. You might consider copying the description from the blog and pasting it here.

10. Set **Availability** of the link.

11. Click on the **Submit** button. The link is added to the page.

You can also create a link to a blog in Course Menu. If you place the link in Course Menu, then the blog should be one that is relevant to all parts of the course. For example, you would probably not place a link to a blog that has been used for just one unit in the course, but you might place a link to the coursewide blog.

To add a link to a blog in Course Menu, perform the following steps:

1. From the **Add Menu Item** menu, select **Create Course Link**:

2. The **Add Course Link** dialog box is displayed. In the **Name** field, enter the name for the link. Students will see this in Course Menu.

3. Click on the **Browse** button. Another pop-up window is displayed, which shows all the assets in the course that you can link to:

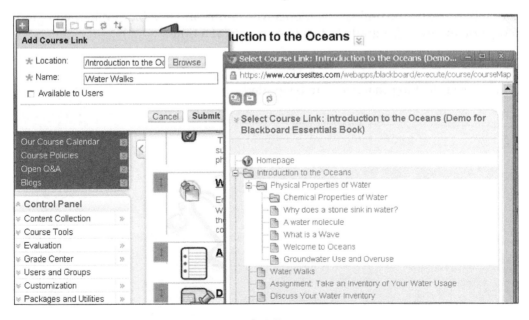

4. Select the blog to which you will link. In our example, we will select **Water Walks**.

5. Mark it as **Available to Users**.

6. To save the link, click on the **Submit** button.

Know the name of the asset that you want to link to.

You can use this technique to link to any asset in your course. Look at the screenshot in step 3 of the preceding procedure, and you'll see that all of the Course Assets show up on the list of possible links. However, they all have the same icon. So, don't depend on being able to tell what kind of asset it is, from this list.

Managing a blog

Now that you have created a blog and your students are posting on it, you can start managing the blog. Blackboard offers several features for this.

Grading blogs

While you are creating a blog, under **Grade Settings** you can assign a number of grade points to the blog. For a forum, you can assign a grade for the entire forum, or just for one thread in the forum. For a blog, you can assign a grade (a number of points) for the entire blog.

There will probably be multiple students who contribute to a blog. When you grade a blog, you are giving a grade to just one student at a time.

To grade a blog, perform the following steps:

1. Select the blog that needs to be graded.

2. From the column on the right-hand side of the screen, select the student to be graded:

3. The system will display all of the entries and comments that the selected person has made in this blog:

4. Click on the **Edit Grade** button.

5. Enter a grade for this student, for this blog:

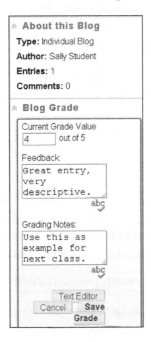

6. The student will see the note that you enter into the **Feedback:** field. It will be displayed, along with the grade, on the student's **My Grades** page:

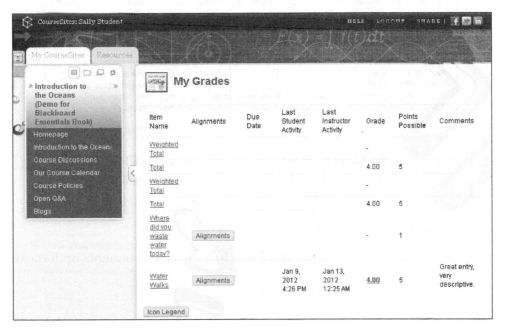

7. The student will not see what you enter into the **Grading Notes:** field. It will be seen only by the teacher. For example, you could use this to leave a note for yourself or for the next teacher.

8. Click on the **Save Grade** button.

Even after saving the grade, you can go back and edit the grade. Just click on the **Edit Grade** button again. The history of the previous grades will be viewable to the instructor.

Later in the book, we'll see how the Grade Center works. From there, you can edit this grade.

Deleting and editing entries and comments

When you created a blog, the settings under **Blog Settings** could be used to enable users to edit and delete their own entries and comments. As the teacher, you can always edit/delete your students' entries/comments.

To edit/delete a blog entry/comment, perform the following steps:

1. While logged in as the teacher, select the blog and then the student.

2. To delete or edit a student's entry, click on the **Menu** icon next to the entry. A pop-up menu appears, with the options—**Edit, Mark as New**, and **Delete**:

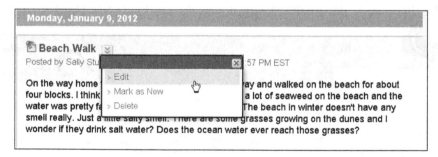

 What happens to comments when you delete a blog entry?
When you delete a blog entry, the comments underneath it are deleted as well.

3. To delete a blog comment:

   ° Click on the **Comments: 2** link to reveal the comments underneath:

○ Click on the **Delete** icon next to the comment that you want to delete:

○ At the pop-up message asking if you want to delete the comment, click on it to confirm the deletion.

 You can delete comments, but you cannot edit them.

When you delete a student's blog entry, and the student returns to the blog, the student might be confused by the missing entry. Instead of deleting blog entries, consider asking the student to edit them. Deleting a student's content can discourage further contributions from that student. If you absolutely must edit or delete the entry yourself, communicate with the student directly and explain why you want to do so. You can also consider replacing the content of the entry with something such as **[This entry deleted by the teacher]**, as shown in the following screenshot:

About wikis

Blackboard enables your students to collaborate on a wiki. A **wiki** is usually a group writing project. While it is rare, you can create a separate wiki for each student. More commonly, you can separate students into groups, and then have a wiki for each group. So each wiki that you create can be for the entire class, for a group within the class, or for an individual.

In this section, we'll see how to create a wiki for the class. Groups are covered in *Chapter 8, Working with Groups*. After you know how to create and manage a class wiki, you will have the background needed to work with group wikis.

Just like every course has a Blogs page that lists all of the blogs in the course, and a Course Discussion page that lists all of the forums in the course, every course has a Wikis page that lists all of the wikis in the course. When you first create a course, a wiki might already be created for you. It depends upon how your administrator has set up the new course template.

Creating a wiki

By itself, the Wikis page is of no use. To give students a wiki, you must create at least one wiki on this page.

To create a wiki, perform the following steps:

1. Select **Course Tools | Wikis**.
2. The page displays all of the wikis in the course. If this is a new course, there are probably no wikis.
3. Click on the **Create Wiki** button. The **Create Wiki** page is displayed.
4. In the **Wiki Information** area, enter the **Name** and **Instructions** fields for the wiki. Students will see the name when the wiki is listed on the Wikis page. They will not see the instructions until they click and select the wiki.
5. In the **Wiki Participation** area, you will determine if students can edit the wiki. Even if you make this wiki available to students, if you don't select **Open to Editing**, then students will be able to see it, but not edit it.
6. For now, make the wiki available, and we'll create a link to it later.
7. Under **Grade Wiki**, you can assign a number of grade points to the wiki.
8. To save your work and create the wiki, click on the **Submit** button.

So I created a wiki. Now what?
If you don't create a link to the wiki, your students will never see it. In a later section, you will see how to create a link to this wiki.

Adding a link to the Wikis page

If you give students a link to the Wikis page, they will see a list of all of the wikis in the course.

To create a link to the Wikis page on **Course Menu**, perform the following steps:

1. From the **Add Menu Item** menu, select **Create Tool Link**:

2. The **Add Tool Link** dialog box is displayed. In the **Name** field, enter the name for the link. Students will see this in Course Menu.
3. From the **Type** drop-down list, select **Wikis**.
4. Mark it as **Available to Users**.
5. To save the link, click on the **Submit** button.

Remember that while the link you create will display whatever name you enter, the Wikis page will always have the title **Wikis** displayed at the top.

To add a link to a wiki to a Content Area, perform the following steps:

1. From **Course Menu**, select a Content Area to which you will add the link.
2. From the **Build Content** menu, select **Add Interactive Tool | Wiki**.
3. The **Create Link: Wiki** page is displayed.
4. Select the **radio** button for **Link to a wiki**.
5. Select the wiki that you want to link to.

6. Click on the **Next** button.

7. Another page is displayed. On this page, you can see the **Name** and **Description** fields for the link. They are copied directly from the wiki. You can leave them as it is, or edit them.

8. In the **Link Name** field, enter the name for the link. This will be displayed to the user. It should already be filled in with the name of the wiki.

9. In the **Text** field, enter a description for the link. It should already be filled in with the description from the wiki. You can edit it or leave it as it is.

10. Set **Availability** of the link.

11. Click on the **Submit** button. The link is added to the page.

Summary

Both blogs and wikis offer a place for your students to build a body of knowledge. Since blog entries are ordered in time, blogs work best when you want the student to document the journey of building their knowledge. However, remember that Blackboard does not give you the ability to automatically gather all the blog entries about a topic in one place. So while it is easy to see the gathering of knowledge over time, it is not as easy to see the final result of that gathering. As wiki entries are organized as per page, they encourage the categorization and organization of knowledge. If seeing the result of the gathering of knowledge is more important than seeing the journey, then consider using a wiki.

One way to take advantage of both tools is to start by using a blog. Have the students blog about an area of study. Encourage (or require) them to read and comment on each other's entries. After students have built a significant body of knowledge in their blogs, make a coursewide wiki available to them. You can start creating pages in the wiki for the categories and subjects that they have blogged about. Then, have the students add their knowledge to the wiki.

In the next chapter, we'll cover the assignments activity.

6
Assignments

In this chapter, we will discuss how to create assignments where the student must submit or upload a material for the instructor to review. You will learn how to review and respond to the files that students submit.

In this chapter, you will learn the following:

- Creating an assignment, which has a file that the student must download
- Receiving notification that a student has submitted a completed assignment
- Grading the assignment
- Sending feedback to the student

About assignments

An **assignment** is essentially an activity where the instructor tells the student, "Go do this, and then submit proof that you've done it". Optional features enable the instructor to supply the student with a file, to upload a file, and to submit both feedback and comments. Blackboard will create a link in the assignment, for the student to upload material to the instructor.

Every assignment must have instructions and a student submission. The instructions are entered by the instructor when (s)he creates the assignment. The student submission can be material that the student types directly into the assignment-feedback form, or something that the student uploads (such as a word document or picture).

The instructor can give a student feedback on the student's submission. In return, the student can give the instructor feedback on the assignment. Instructors can also allow multiple submissions, so the student has multiple tries to get it right. No matter how many trials the student takes, or how many files the student uploads, the instructor will give only one grade to the student.

Adding an assignment

To add an assignment to a Content Page, follow these steps:

1. Select the Content Page to which you want to add an assignment.

2. Select **Create Assessment | Assignment**. The **Create Assignment** page is displayed.

3. Both the **Name** and the **Instructions** fields that you enter will be displayed on the page with the assignment, as shown in the following screenshot:

Take an Inventory of Your Water Usage

Attached Files: Water Inventory Assignment.rtf (66.63 KB)

Download the form for this assignment. Use it to record approximately how much water you use at home each day. Do this for four consecutive days, then upload the form back into this assignment.

> In the preceding example, the instructor tells the student to download a file. You might want to remind the students to create a folder on their computers to hold all the material that they download from the course.

4. Under **Attached Files**, you can add any files that you want the student to download and use in the assignment (this is optional). These can be files that you want the student to modify and then upload (such as a form to fill out), or files that contain instructions for an activity (such as instructions for performing an experiment), or source files that the student will use to create something (such as some raw video footage).

   If the student will complete the assignment while (s)he is online, enter the instructions into the **Instructions** area as shown earlier. If the student will complete the assignment while (s)he is offline, consider supplying the student with printer-friendly instructions that (s)he can download.

   Blackboard will allow the student to upload files up to 100 MB in size.

5. The **Grading** and **Availability** sections contain standard options.

6. If you enter **Due Date** for the assignment, it will not appear on the Content Page (see the preceding screenshot). However, it will appear in several other places. When the student enters the assignment, the due date will appear on the assignment page:

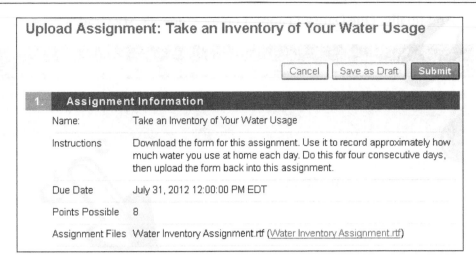

The due date will also appear in the student's **To Do** block. Usually, the **To Do** block is added to the course's home page, and also to the student's home page. In the following screenshot, you can see the assignment in the **To Do** block of the course's home page. Because it was recently added, you can also see the assignment in the **What's New** block:

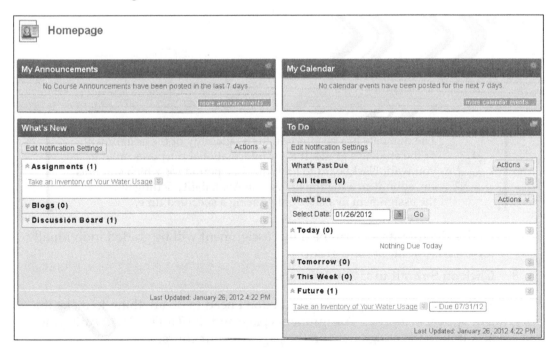

And finally, **Due Date** will appear on the student's **My Grades** page:

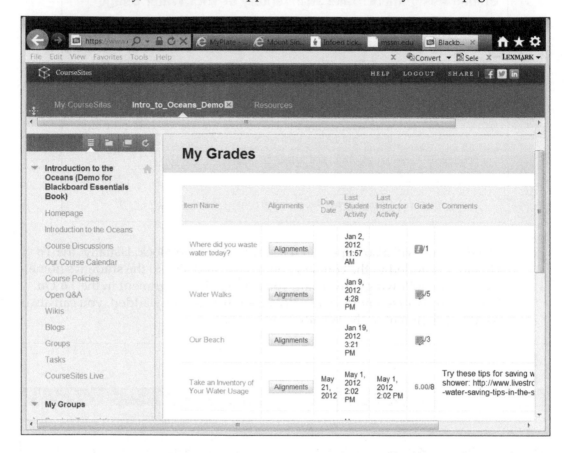

 The due date has no effect on the availability of the assignment, or the student's grade. It is for informational purposes only. If you want Blackboard to limit the time period for which students can submit an assignment, use the Availability setting to make the assignment available only during a specified time.

7.   Under **Recipients**, determine if this assignment will be graded individually for each student, or for a group.

8.   Click on **Submit** to save your work.

The assignment is added to the course. You don't need to do anything to make the assignment appear within the **Assignments** page and the **To Do** block. And, you can create a link to the assignment on the pages of your course.

Responding to an assignment

Most of this book is written from the course creator's and instructor's point of view. But in this section, we will see an assignment from the student's point of view. This will enable you to determine how the choices you make while creating the assignment will affect your students' experience.

Not all assignments will require the student to download or upload files. However, these instructions include these steps so that you can see a more complete example of a student's experience:

1. Select the assignment. You might select it from Content Page that the assignment appears on; or select it from the **To Do** block, or the **What's New** block.

2. The student sees **Name**, **Instructions**, **Due Date**, **Points Possible** (if any), and **Assignment Files** (if any).

 If the assignment has files that the student must download, consider mentioning this explicitly in the instructions, asking the student to click on the file to download it. Then there will be no doubt that the student knows how to start the assignment.

3. In our example, the student clicks on the assignment file. Note that the way in which the download happens will vary, based on the student's browser. For example, Internet Explorer will usually launch a pop-up window showing the download's progress, while Google Chrome will usually add a tab at the bottom of the browser window, showing the download's progress:

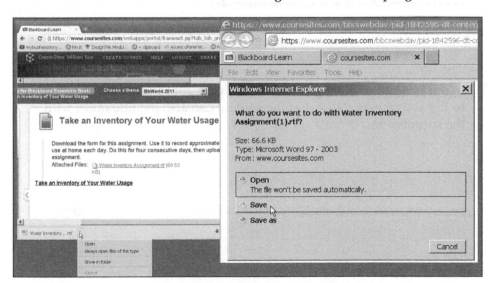

4. The student will usually work on the file outside of Blackboard. To make it easier for the student, include the instructions for using that file in another file; that is, when the student downloads the file, (s)he should also be downloading the instructions for using the file:

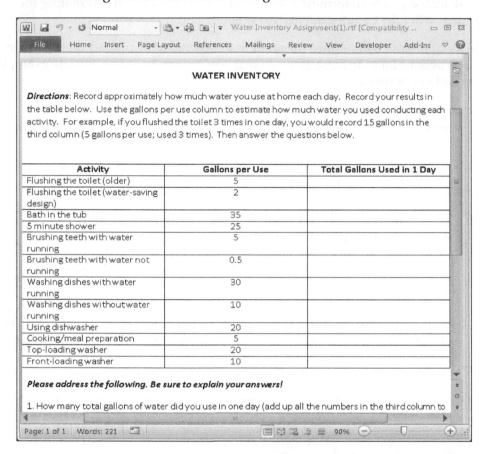

5. In our example, the student will modify the file, and then upload it to the assignment. Note that the student can also include notes with the submission:

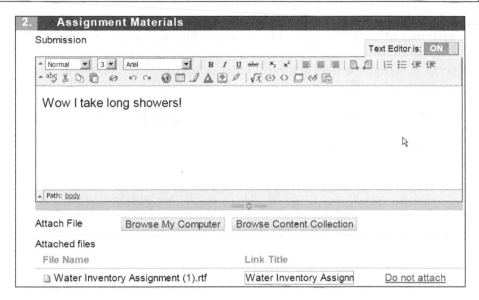

6. Student submissions appear in the instructor's Grade Center, under **Needs Grading**:

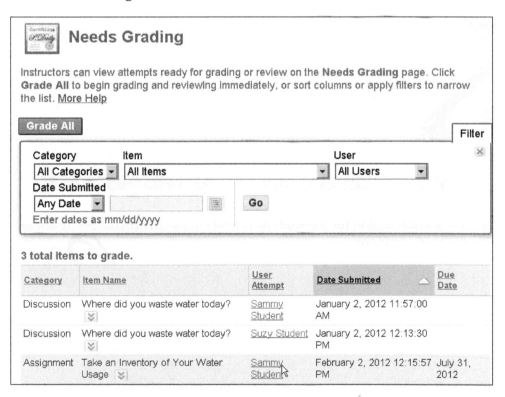

7. When the instructor clicks on the student's name, the grading page for that assignment is displayed. In this window, the instructor can offer feedback on that submission. Near the bottom of the page, there is an **Instructor Notes** section, where the instructor can enter notes that are visible only to the instructors of this course:

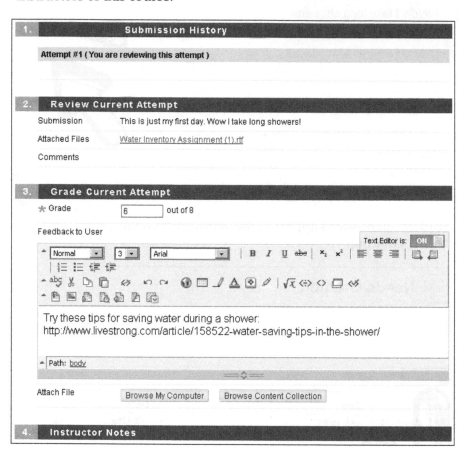

8. The **Grade** section for the student appears in the **Instructor Feedback** area of the assignment:

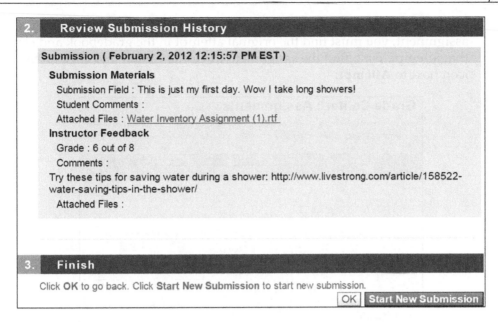

Note that at this point, the student can start a new submission for the assignment. This is because, when the instructor created the assignment, (s)he allowed multiple submissions on the **Creating Assignment** page:

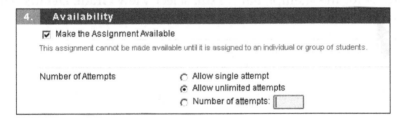

As you can see, an assignment that allows multiple submissions gives the instructor and student a chance to collaborate on the student's success. Allowing multiple attempts also enables the student to resubmit in case (s)he uploads the wrong file the first time.

If you allow only a single attempt, and the student needs to resubmit the assignment, you must find the original attempt in the gradebook and clear that attempt. First, find the assignment in **Grade Center** and click on the icon next to **Attempt**:

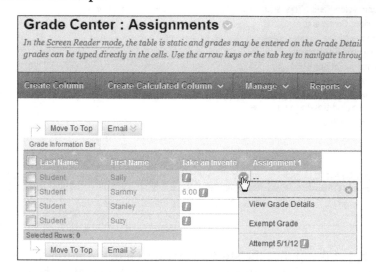

9. From this pop-up menu, select **View Grade Details**. In our example, there is no grade for the attempt, but we still select **View Grade Details**. This brings up a window where all the attempts for this assignment are listed:

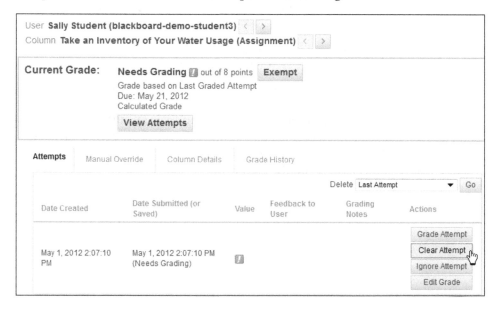

10. Click on the **Clear Attempt** button to delete the attempt from the record.

Summary

In this example, we had a student download a file, work with it, and then upload the file into an assignment. But remember that assignments don't need to be done online. An assignment can also be done in the real, physical world. For example, you could instruct your students to build something and then bring it to class. Or, you could instruct them to make a video and upload it to another site, or contribute to www.wikipedia.org. The student doesn't need to upload anything for you to be able to grade the assignment because Blackboard's Grade Center enables you to give a grade to any assignment at any time. So whenever you need to instruct your students to perform some kind of independent action, consider using an assignment.

In the next chapter, we'll learn how to build and use tests.

7
Testing Students

Blackboard includes a robust testing feature. It is a flexible feature, so you can use tests as an assessment, and as a teaching tool.

Blackboard enables you to add several kinds of questions to your tests. You can also add media and descriptive pages. You can control the page breaks in a test, and create several kinds of feedback. All of these features are covered in this chapter. You could complete these steps in a different order. For example, you could create questions first, create the test, and then add the questions to the test. The process here is a common and easily understood method.

In this chapter, you will learn about the following:

- Creating a blank test
- Creating new questions
- Organizing questions into question pools
- Adding random blocks of questions to a test
- Adding question sets to a test
- Determining when to use random blocks, rather than question sets

Creating a test

Creating a test is a multipart process. The first part is to create a blank test. Next, you determine the behavior of questions using Test Question Settings. The next part is to create questions and add them to the test, using Test Canvas. The fourth part is to add the test to your course, and select settings for that occurrence of the test.

Creating a blank test

In this part of the process, you will create a blank test. Later, the test will need to be populated with questions and added to a page:

1. Navigate to the Content Page where you want to add the test.

2. Select **Create Assessment | Test**. The **Create Test** page is displayed.

3. Under the **Add Test** section, you can either select a test that has already been created in this course, or create a new test. In this example, we will select the **Create** button.

4. The **Test Information** page is displayed.

5. The **Name** and **Description** fields will be displayed on any page to which you add the test.

6. The **Instructions** field will be displayed after a student selects and enters the test.

7. Click on the **Submit** button. The **Test Canvas** page is displayed.

Determining the behavior of questions by using Question Settings

The Question Settings page determines how individual questions behave:

1. Click on the **Question Settings** button. The **Test Question Settings** page is displayed.

2. Selecting **Provide feedback for individual answers** enables you to create different feedback, which will be displayed to the student, for each answer of each question. You can use the feedback to explain why an answer is correct or incorrect. This is a good option if you want to make the test a learning experience.

3. The setting for **Add images, files, and external links to questions** enables you to attach these items to the questions. The setting for **Add images, files, and external links to answers** enables students to attach the items to their answers.

4. The **Question Metadata** setting enables you to add descriptive information to your questions. Students will never see this metadata. However, instructors will see it. This metadata can be used when instructors are searching for questions. In the following example, the instructor has assigned a category and a level of difficulty to a question:

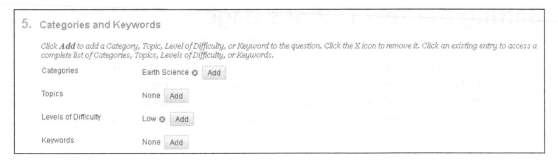

5. Under **Scoring,** you can specify the default points for each question in the test. However, you can change the number of points that each question is worth.

6. If you enable the setting for **Specify random ordering of answers**, be careful about writing answers like "All of the above", because the order of the answers will change.

7. To save your changes, click on the **Submit** button. This returns you to the **Test Canvas** page. You are now ready to create and add questions.

Adding and creating questions on Test Canvas

The process for creating questions changes according to the kind of question you are creating. In a later section, we will cover this process. Once you've created questions, you can then present them in random groups:

1. To create a new question, select **Create Question**, and then select the type of question you want to create. For more information about how to create questions, see the section *Creating Questions*, later in this chapter.

2. If you want to use randomized questions, see the section *Random Blocks versus Question Sets*, later in this chapter.

3. Save your test. You now have a complete test. However, it is not being displayed to the students.

Adding the test to a page in your course

You need to add the test to a page in your course so that students can access it:

1. To add the test to a Content Page, select **Assessments | Test**. On the **Add Test** page, select the test, and click on the **Submit** button.

2. The **Test Options** page is displayed. The **Name** and **Description** fields that you enter here will be displayed to the students.

Setting the Test Options page

The most common test options are implemented as follows:

1. Under **Test Availability**, you can choose **Add a New Announcement for this Test**. If you enable this, an announcement that you have added the test will appear in the **Announcements** block for the student. Note that it won't have the due date of the test, but just an announcement that it was added:

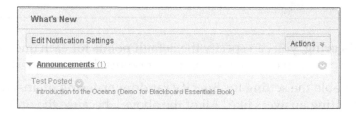

2. Under **Due Date**, if you select the checkbox and enter a date, the due date will be added to the student's **To Do** list:

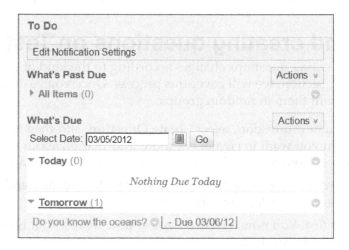

3. Under **Self-assessment Options**, if you remove the check mark from **Include this Test in Grade Center Score Calculations**, then this test will only be for self assessment. It will not be counted towards the student's grade for the course. The instructor cannot see the student's answers.

4. Set the other options as desired, and then click on **Submit**.

Note that **Test Options** appears only when a test is added to a page.

Specific instructions for some of these steps are given in the sections that follow.

Creating questions

Blackboard enables you to create many types of questions. The process for creating these questions is similar for all types. Some details change, based on the type of question. In the following screenshot, you can see the types of questions that Blackboard supports:

In this section, we will look at what is common to the process of creating all types of questions.

Navigating to the Test Canvas page

The **Test Canvas** page is where you add existing, and create new, questions.

If you are in the middle of creating a test, and you want to create a new question for that test, you are probably at the Test Canvas page. If so, perform the following steps:

1. Select the **Create Question** drop-down list.

    If you are not currently creating the test, you need to reopen the test before you can add questions to it.

2. From the main menu, select **Course Tools** | **Tests, Surveys, and Pools**. From the drop-down next to the test, select **Edit**.

Enter the type, title, and question text

Options such as type, title, and question text are universal for almost all question types, and can be entered as follows:

1. From the **Create Question** drop-down list, select the type of question that you are creating. The **Create Question** page will be displayed.

2. Enter the **Question Title** field for the question. When instructors select questions to add to tests, and see the grade reports for the questions, the instructor will see this title.

3. Enter the **Question Text** field. This is the question itself, which the students will see.

4. Immediately below **Question Text**, you will see fields for **File**, **Action**, **External Link**, and **Link Name**:

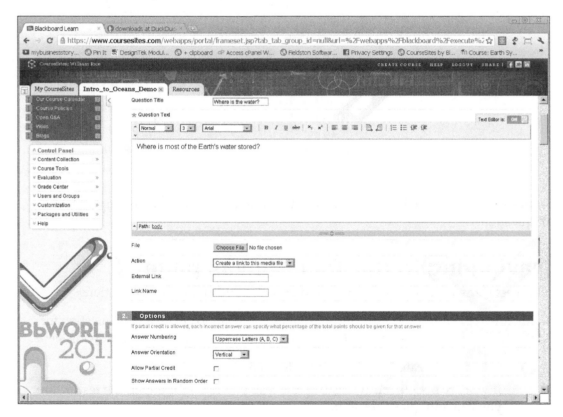

5. Note that you can attach a file to this question. If you do so, Blackboard will either display a link to the file, or display the file on the page with the question text. The **Action** drop-down determines whether the system displays a link or the actual file.

6. If you add **External Link** to this question, Blackboard places the link below the question text. The link name is entered in the **Link Name** field.

 Further down the page, under each answer, and also under each bit of feedback, you will again see the fields for **File**, **Action**, **External Link**, and **Link Name**. If you fill these in as an answer, they are displayed along with that answer. The student sees the file or link while looking at the answers. If you fill these in for feedback, the student sees them only if (s)he submits the corresponding answer. Make sure you know whether you are adding files and links to an answer, or to an answer's feedback.

Adding answers and answer feedback

For most types of questions, you enter answers that the student chooses or that are compared to the answer that the student enters; for example, True/False, Multiple Choice, Jumbled Sentence, and Matching. This section is for these types of questions. Other types of questions don't have a list of answers that the student chooses from; for example, Paragraph. If the question you are creating doesn't have **Answer** and **Feedback** fields, skip this section.

1. Under the **Options** section, there are several options that affect the behavior of the question.

2. **Answer Numbering** determines if the answers will be numbered or lettered.

3. **Answer Orientation** determines if the answers will be listed across the page (horizontally) or one after the other (vertically). If you intend to deliver this course on a device with a small screen, consider listing the answers vertically to avoid horizontal scrolling.

4. If this is a multiple-choice question, you can choose **Allow Partial Credit** for some answers.

5. If you choose **Show Answers in Random Order**, beware of creating questions with answers like "All of the above" or "The first two choices".

6. For **Number of Answers**, you are choosing how many answers to display in the editor, and not how many answers the question will have. The question will show as many answers as you will fill on this page. You can choose to display eight spaces for answers on this page, but if you fill in only three of them, the question will show three answers.

7. If there is a question where the user chooses an answer(s) from a list, then each answer will have a radio button or checkbox next to it. On the first answer, this is labeled **Correct**. Use this to indicate what the correct answer(s) is.

8. The **Answers** field contains the answer that the student will see. Notice that the editor enables you to enter and format text and equations for the answer:

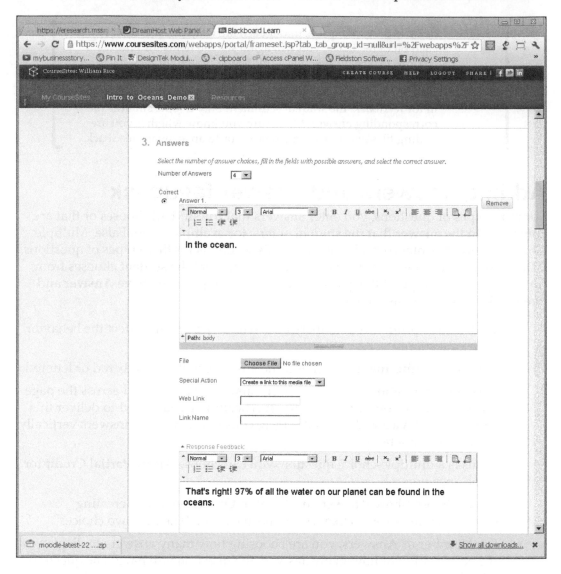

9. Under **Answers**, you see fields for **File**, **Action**, **External Link**, and **Link Name**. If you fill these in for an answer, they are displayed along with that answer. The student sees the file or link while looking at the answers. By default, you cannot insert a link or image directly into the answer (note that the text editor for the **Answers** field doesn't have icons to insert them). But you can attach a link, image, or other file using these fields:

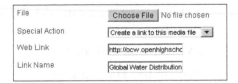

 You can enable the ability to insert images and links directly into questions and answers, under **Question Settings**. While on the **Test Canvas** page, look for this button in the upper-right corner of the page:

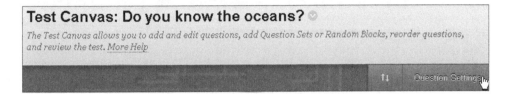

10. If there is a **Response Feedback** field, enter the feedback for this answer.

11. Once again, you will see the fields for **File**, **Action**, **External Link**, and **Link Name**. If you fill them in as a response, then they are displayed along with that response's feedback.

12. In the **Feedback** section of the question, you can create feedback that is displayed when any correct and/or incorrect answer is selected. These are especially useful for explaining the relevance of a question.

Adding categories, keywords, and notes

A common feature of questions is that you can tag them with metadata; that is, you can add information about the questions, such as category, topic, and keywords, as follows:

1. Under the **Categories and Keywords** section, you will see buttons for **Categories**, **Topics**, **Levels of Difficulty**, and **Keywords**. Adding these features makes it easier for yourself and others to find this question later.

 Consider working with your site administrator and other users to develop categories, topics, and keywords that are meaningful to all the users in your organization. This information becomes more useful when everyone agrees on the meanings.

2. Under the **Instructor Notes** section, you can add notes that only other instructors will see. Students will not see this information.

3. To save your work, click on the **Submit** button.

4. Blackboard takes you back to the **Test Canvas** page. The question that you just added is displayed on the page:

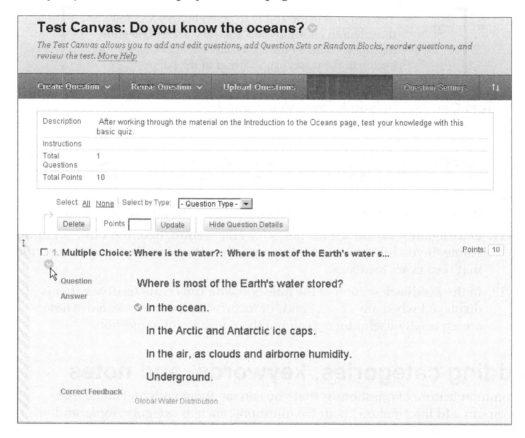

5. You can continue adding questions, or go back to edit this question by clicking on the "check" sign next to it.

Other types of questions

The preceding example showed you a multiple-choice question. It demonstrated the common features of Blackboard test questions. The following sections tell you about some of the other types of questions available.

Calculated formula questions

A **calculated formula** presents the student with a formula to solve. For each student, it can present different values for the variables. For example, a calculated formula question about the Pythagorean formula, could look similar to the following screenshot:

The variables in this question, 3 and 2, could be different for each student. Blackboard would calculate the correct answer for each set of unique variables.

Before we look at the step-by-step directions for creating a calculated formula, let's look at the individual pieces of the question. After we understand the pieces, we'll put them together into a finished question.

Suppose that we are testing our students on the Pythagorean theorem. We want to test the students on the following formula:

$$a^2 + b^2 = c^2$$

We'll ask Blackboard to substitute values for the variables, so that our students are presented with these formulas, as follows:

$$3^2 + 4^2 = c^2 \text{ and } 5^2 + 12^2 = c^2 \text{ and } 8^2 + 15^2 = c^2$$

Notice that Blackboard substituted values for the variables a and b. We will ask the students to solve for c.

When you create a calculated formula question, you first write the question that the student will read. The question must contain the names of the variables that Blackboard will give values to. In our example, the question text must contain the variables a and b. So while creating the question, we would enter the following:

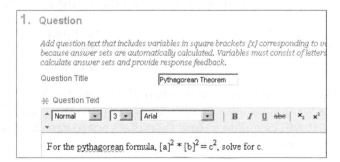

And when the question is displayed, the student will see a page similar to the following screenshot:

Notice that when we entered the question text, we put a and b in brackets:

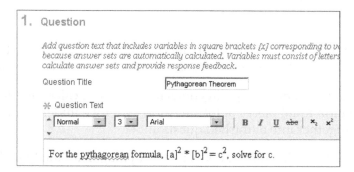

When we put a variable in brackets, we are telling Blackboard that we want the system to replace that variable with a value. In the preceding example, when the system displayed the question, it replaced a with 3 and b with 2.

Notice also that the text which is not in brackets is displayed normally. The variable c is not in brackets, so the system does not give it any special treatment. It's just text.

We just established that when we put a variable in brackets, we are indicating that we want Blackboard to replace that variable with a value. But what value? While we are creating our question, we will specify a minimum and maximum value for each variable.

After we write the text of the question, we must give Blackboard the formula for calculating the answer. Whatever values Blackboard uses for the variables, when it plugs them into the formula we give, the result should be the correct answer.

Again, here is our equation: $a^2 + b^2 = c^2$. Blackboard will plug in values for a and b. It will then calculate c^2. However, we don't want the student to enter c^2. We aren't asking the student to calculate c^2. We are asking the student to calculate c.

So how do we write the equation so that, when given a and b, Blackboard calculates the value of c? It is written as: $\sqrt{a^2 + b^2}$. With this equation, when Blackboard plugs in values for a and b, it will calculate c. And then Blackboard can check the answer that the student enters against its calculation.

This is called Answer Formula. While creating our question, we will need to enter this formula.

Let's look at the procedure step-by-step:

1. From the **Create Question** drop-down list, select **Calculated Formula**. The **Create Question** page will be displayed.

2. Enter **Title** for the question. When instructors select questions to add to tests, and when they see grade reports for questions, they see the question's title.

3. Enter **Question Text**. This is the question itself, which the students will see. When you enter the question text, put the variables that you want Blackboard to replace, in brackets:

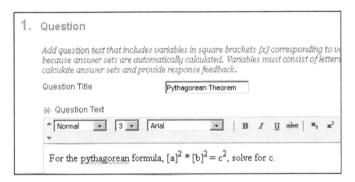

4. Immediately below **Question Text**, you will see a field for **Answer Formula**. In this field, create the formula that Blackboard will use to calculate the answer:

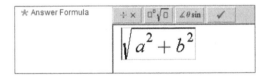

In Question Text, which you declared to Blackboard, these letters in brackets will be the variables. In Answer Formula, you gave Blackboard the formula that it will plug those variables into, and calculate the answer.

5. Under **Options**, you will specify the following:

How close to the correct answer the student must be, to get full credit:

Whether you will allow partial credit:

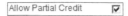

If you do allow partial credit, then how close to the correct answer the student must be to get partial credit:

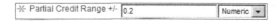

If the student gets partial credit, what percentage of the full credit the student will get:

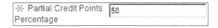

6.   Click on the **Next** button to proceed to the next page:

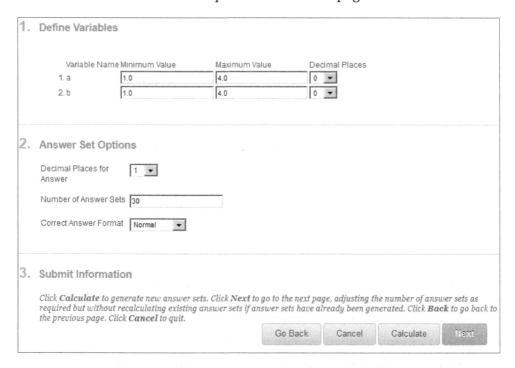

7.   Under **Define Variables**, set **Minimum Value** and **Maximum Value** for the variable that you entered into Question Text. Also set the number of **Decimal Places for Answer** allowed. When Blackboard presents the question to the student, it will substitute values that are within the range you specify here for the variables.

8. Under **Answer Set Options**, one of the things you will specify is how many unique combinations of variables Blackboard will generate. In the next step, you will see all of the combinations that are generated, and have the chance to delete any that you do not want.

9. Click on the **Calculate** button to generate the values for the variables:

Note that the answers are specified as X.X ± 0. The ± 0 means that the system requires an exact answer. This was specified on the first page of the question, under **Options**, in the field labeled **Answer Range**. If you want to change this, you can use the **Go Back** button to return to that page and change the tolerance for the answer.

10. If there are any combinations that you do not want to present to the student, click on the **Remove** button to remove them.

11. Under the **Feedback** section, you can enter feedback for the correct and incorrect answers.

12. Under the **Categories and Keywords** section, you will see buttons for **Categories**, **Topics**, **Levels of Difficulty**, and **Keywords**. You can use them to add metadata to your question.

13. Under the **Instructor Notes** section, you can add notes that only other instructors will see. Students will not see this information.

14. To save your work, click on the **Submit** button.

Calculated numeric

When presented with a calculated numeric question, the student must answer with a number. But unlike the calculated formula question, all students will see the same formula with the same numbers. Therefore, the correct answer will be the same for all the students.

Either/Or—True/False, Yes/No, Right/Wrong, Correct/Incorrect

This option can be used to create a True/False, Yes/No, Right/Wrong, or Correct/ Incorrect question. If you need to create a question that has only two choices, and you cannot use the answers given here, then you'll need to create a multiple-choice question and write your own answers.

Essay

The Essay question presents the student with a **Question** and **Text** field to enter an answer. Alternatively, it can present a sample answer. It must be graded manually. The student can type into the **Answer** field, or copy the answer from another document and paste it into the **Answer** field.

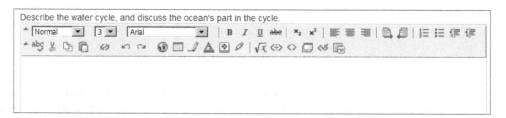

If you want the student to submit something that (s)he has already written, consider using a File Response question instead. Then, the student can just upload the document, instead of copying and pasting its contents.

File Response

Students answer a File Response question by uploading a file from their computer, or from Content Collection. It is graded manually.

A student can upload any kind of file, and not just file types that are recognized by Blackboard. In this case, Blackboard is just the tool that carries the file to the instructor. Think of it as similar to an attachment for an e-mail message.

Filling in the Blank and Multiple Blanks

In Blank and Multiple Blank questions, you write question text that has one or more blanks. The student must type the correct answer(s) into these blank(s).

When you create the question, you specify where the blanks are using brackets, as shown in the following screenshot:

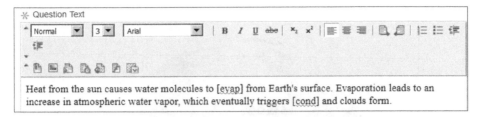

In the preceding example, we created two variables. One is called **evap** and the other is called **cond**. While creating the question, we will specify the correct answers for these variables. In the following example, note that we entered a common misspelling for the variable as the correct answer:

To the student, the question will look similar to what is shown in the following screenshot:

Heat from the sun causes water molecules to [ ] from Earth's surface. Evaporation leads to an increase in atmospheric water vapor, which eventually triggers [ ] and clouds form.

Hot Spot

A **Hot Spot** question presents the student with some question text in the Question Test field and an image. The student must click on the correct area of the image.

When creating this type of question, you will upload the image. Then, you will drag your mouse on top of the image to specify the hot spot. A hot spot must be a rectangle; no other shapes can be specified. There can be only one hot spot in the question.

As you drag your mouse to create the hot spot, Blackboard shows you the coordinates. From this, you can see how large the hot spot is, in pixels:

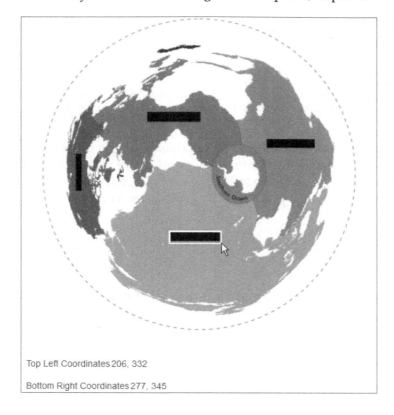

Top Left Coordinates 206, 332

Bottom Right Coordinates 277, 345

In the preceding example, the hot spot is 71 pixels wide and 13 pixels high. Most desktop monitors display between 96 and 120 pixels per inch. On most desktop monitors, this hot spot would be about 0.7 inches wide and 0.13 inches high. When creating a Hot Spot question, determine how large the image and the hot spot will be for your intended students. Will it be large enough so that your students can accurately click on the hot spot with the first click? You can use the following list of pixel sizes to determine what size of your images and hot spots will be shown: http://en.wikipedia.org/wiki/List_of_displays_by_pixel_density.

Jumbled Sentence

A **Jumbled Sentence** question displays a sentence with one or more drop-down lists embedded in the sentence. The user selects the correct word from the drop-down list. Some systems call this a cloze question.

Matching

In a **Matching** question, the student must match items in one column to items in another column. You can include different numbers of questions and answers. It looks similar to what is shown in the following screenshot:

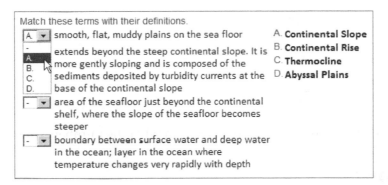

Multiple Answer and Multiple Choice

The **Multiple Choice** question requires the student to select one correct answer. **Multiple Answer** questions allow the student to select one or several correct answers.

In a multiple-choice question, you can allow partial credit. The partial credit for all of the correct answers must add up to 100 percent.

In a multiple-answer question, you can allow partial credit. In this case, the student would need to select all of the correct answers to get 100 percent. Your question will probably end with something such as "Select all the answers that apply".

In a multiple-answer question, you can also specify that several answers are 100% correct. In this case, the student would need to select just one of the correct answers to get 100%. Your question will probably end with something such as "Select any that apply".

Opinion Scale/Likert

Opinion Scale/Likert question is most often seen on surveys. Students choose an answer from a scale, which runs from lesser to greater. It could read something like, "For this statement, choose whether you: disagree strongly, disagree somewhat, agree somewhat, or agree strongly". While these questions are rarely used on tests, they are popular for surveys.

Ordering

The **Ordering** question type asks the student to place items in the correct order. The student does this by selecting numbers from the drop-down lists next to each item:

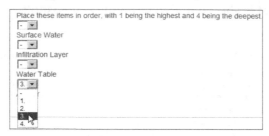

When writing Question Text, be sure to explain what the numbers mean.

Quiz Bowl

Quiz Bowl questions can be fun, but also difficult to write. You give the student an answer, and the student must respond by writing a question for that answer. For example, you might give the student an answer such as "ions". Then, you might expect the student to submit a question such as "What are charged atoms called?"

Quiz Bowl questions can be difficult to write because they are graded by the system. Therefore, you must tell the system what words and phrases you are looking for in the student's answer. The trick is to give the student an answer whose question is very specific. For example, suppose you gave the answer "rip current"; there is so much the student could write about rip currents, that it would be difficult to specify all of the key words and phrases that apply to it. In general, if the student is to write a long paragraph about a term or phrase, don't use that term or phrase as an answer to a Quiz Bowl. Limit the answers to items that have short definitions and very specific usage in your course.

Short Answer

A **Short Answer** question is like an essay question in two ways: the student enters (or pastes) the answer into a textbox. And, it must be evaluated manually by the instructor. The difference is that a Short Answer question requires you to specify the number of rows in the textbox that the student uses.

Random blocks versus question sets

While creating a test, you can choose to add a random block of questions, and/or a question set. Both features enable you to add a group of questions all at once. However, they meet different teaching needs.

Before we talk about the difference between a question set and random block, let's look at the similarities:

- Both consist of a group of questions that you specify
- In both cases, when you add them to a test, you specify how many of the questions from the group the test should display
- Both give you an easy way to add a specific group of questions to a test, to randomize questions, and to reuse that group of questions on other tests

What is the difference then? Simply put, the main difference between random blocks and question sets, is the source of their questions.

Question pools, the source for random blocks

A **question pool** is a group of questions that are chosen from the course. You can filter the questions using multiple criteria. In the following screenshot, you can see the search criteria, which you can use when looking for questions to add to a pool to various categories—**Pools**, **Tests**, **Question types**, **Categories**, **Topics**, **Levels of Difficulty**, and **Keywords**:

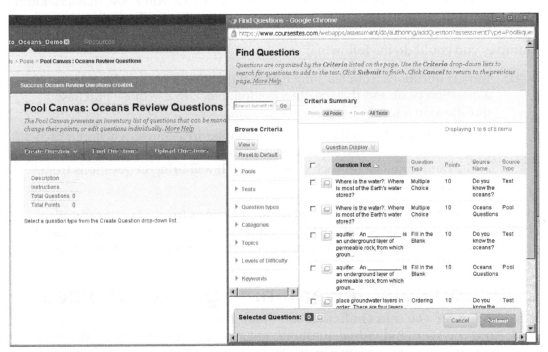

A question pool can be exported out of your Blackboard system, and imported into another system. This makes them a good tool for sharing questions among Blackboard systems. Also, when you upload a batch of questions into Blackboard, you can upload them directly into a question pool. For example, if you purchase learning material and test questions from a vendor, you can upload the purchased questions into a question pool, so you will always know their source.

A question pool uses criteria to find a question from anywhere in your course. After finding questions, you select them individually for the pool. Until you deploy a pool in a test, you can change the questions that are in it. However, once a random block or question set that uses a question pool is deployed, the question pool can no longer be edited.

Now that we know more about question pools, let's clearly state the relationship between a question pool and a random block.

A random block will display a specified number of questions, from a selected question pool or pools.

In the previous section, we said that the main difference between random blocks and question sets is the source of their questions. Now that you know that a random block gets its questions from a pool(s), you can see that this is a limitation of random blocks. However, it can also make it easier to organize and reuse questions. For example, you could do the following:

1. Import questions from teaching material that you have purchased into a question pool, and then create a random block to use those purchased questions in a test.

2. Create a review test at the end of each chapter in a course. Then, put each chapter's questions into a question pool for that chapter. For the final test, add a random block for each chapter, which will bring in questions from that chapter's question pool.

In general, a **random block** is a method to put questions from a specific question pool(s) into a test. Use question pools to organize your questions into meaningful groups, and then use a random block to add questions from the pools to a test.

Question sets: fewer limits, greater choices

In a question set, you select individual questions from anywhere, not just from a pool. And, you select individual questions, not a pool. Until you deploy the question set, you can remove and add questions. After you've added all the questions you want for the set, add the set to a test and specify the number of questions you want to appear.

The following screenshot shows the user creating a question set. Notice that the question set allows the user to pull questions from any pool, and any other test in the course. There is also all the other search criteria that you have when creating a question pool:

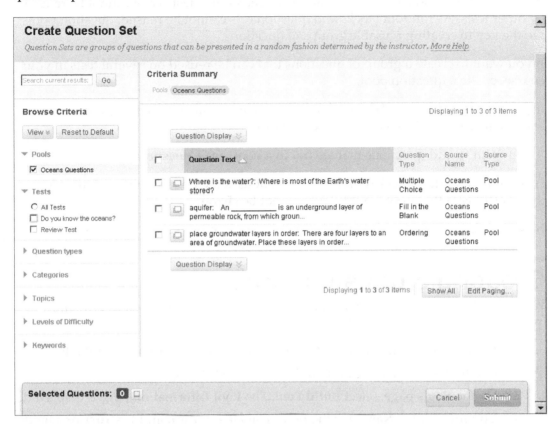

With a random block, you must first create a question pool to find the questions you want. Then, you add a random block to the test, which displays a specified number of questions from the question pool. With a question set, you do both of these at once. When you add the question set to a test, you use the preceding criteria to find the questions. You also specify how many of the questions to display to each student.

Which should I use: Random Block or Question Set?

In the following sections, you will see how to add random blocks and question sets to a course. But first, let's consider what we learned about question pools, random blocks, and question sets.

A question pool enables you to find questions from all over your course. It can be used as a source of questions in both random blocks and in question sets. It can be reused many times in a course.

A random block and a question set are both created in a test. They cannot be reused by other tests. As random blocks and question sets cannot be reused, question pools are the key to creating reusable groups of questions.

If you want to create a group of questions that can be reused on several tests in your course, create a question pool.

If you want to add a number of questions from an organized pool of questions to a test, the fastest way is to create a random block.

If you want to add questions that are not in a pool, use a question set.

As soon as a random block or question set that uses the pool is deployed in a test, the questions in that pool are set. They cannot be changed.

Now, let's learn how to create question pools, random blocks, and question sets.

Creating a question pool

When you build a question pool, you can create new questions or select existing questions to add to the pool as follows:

1. From the main menu, select **Course Tools | Tests, Surveys, and Pools**.
2. On the **Tests, Surveys, and Pools** page, select **Pools**.
3. On the **Pools** page, select **Build Pool**. The **Pool Information** page is displayed.
4. You must enter **Name** for the pool. The **Description** and **Instructions** fields are optional. These three items will be seen by the instructors, but not by the students.

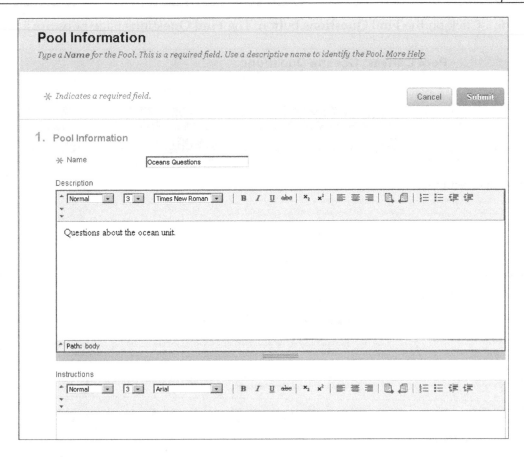

5. Click on the **Submit** button. The **Pool Canvas: Oceans Questions** page is displayed. On this page, you can do the following:

   ° Create new questions and add them to the pool. If you want to create a new question for the pool, select **Create Question**. There is more information about creating questions in a previous section, *Creating Questions*. Note that the questions you create for this pool are affected by Question Settings, which are accessed by clicking on the **Question Settings** button in the upper-right corner of the screen. For more information about Question Settings, see the *Using Question Settings to determine the behavior of questions* section, earlier in this chapter.

   ° Upload questions from another system, into the pool. These instructions will not cover uploading questions.

   ° Find existing questions and add them to the pool. To find existing questions to add to the pool, continue with the following steps.

6. Click on the **Find Questions** button. The **Find Questions** page pops up:

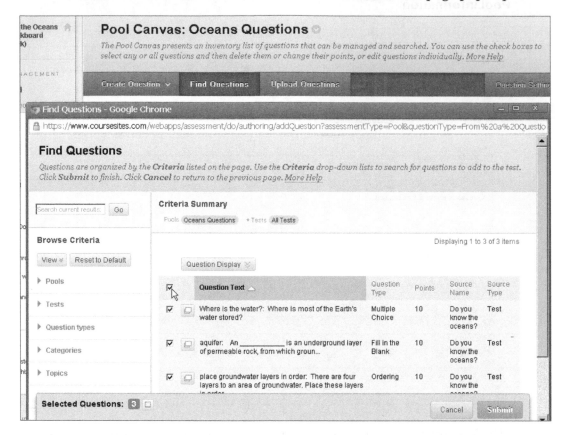

7. You can use several criteria to find questions for the pool. This includes searching other question pools. Select search criteria to display the questions that you want to include.

8. Click on the checkbox next to the questions that you want to include.

9. Click on the **Submit** button. You are returned to the Question Pool canvas page. On this page, you will see **Number of Questions**, which you added to the pool.

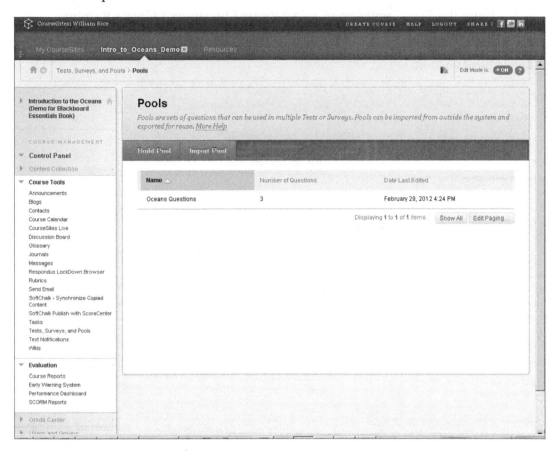

The question pool is created, and ready for use. Remember that once this pool is added to a test and after the test is deployed, you cannot change the questions in the pool.

Creating a random block

A random block is created while you are editing a test:

1. From the **Test Canvas** page, select **Reuse Questions | Create Random Block**. The **Create Random Block** page is displayed as follows:

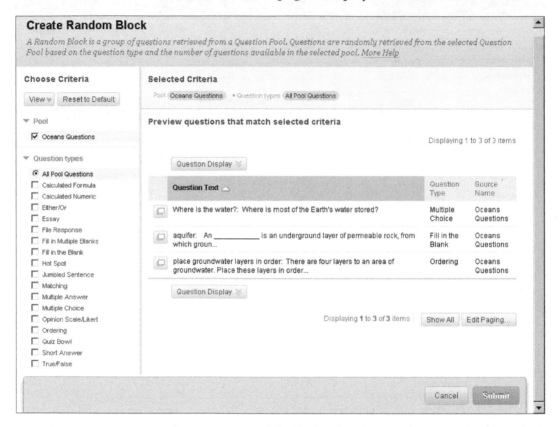

2. Click to place a check mark next to the pool or pools that you want to draw questions from. You must select at least one pool.

3. Select the question types that you want to draw from.

4. The results of your search are listed on the right-hand side of the page. Select the questions that you want to include in the random block.

5. Click on the **Submit** button. You are returned to the **Test Canvas** page. The random block is displayed on this page:

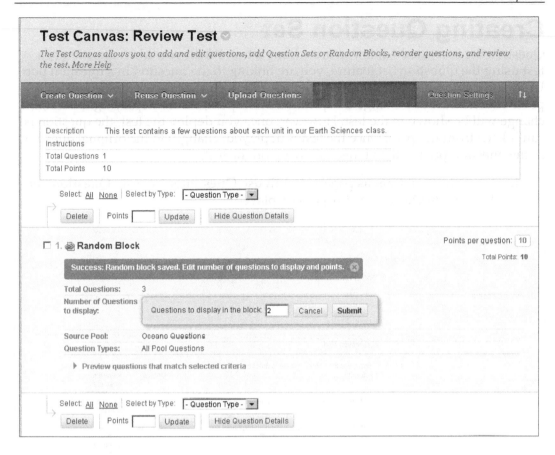

6. The **Total Questions** field tells you how many questions are in the block. The **Total Points** field tells you how many points all the questions are worth, taken together. You can change the number of questions the block displays, and the number of points per question.

Note that when you create a random block, you don't need to give it a name or description. This is because this block will not exist outside of the test. It exists only on this test.

Creating Question Set

Question Set is created while you are editing a test. When you add a question to a test using the Question Set feature, you are linking to the question in a question pool. Until you deploy the test, the question does not exist in the test. It exists only in the pool. Therefore, if you change the question in the pool, before deploying the test, the change will be shown in the test. However, once you deploy the test, the question is "unlinked" from the pool. Once the test is deployed, changes to the original question in the question pool will no longer show up on the test:

1. From the **Test Canvas** page, select **Reuse Questions | Create Question Set**. The Create Question Set page is displayed:

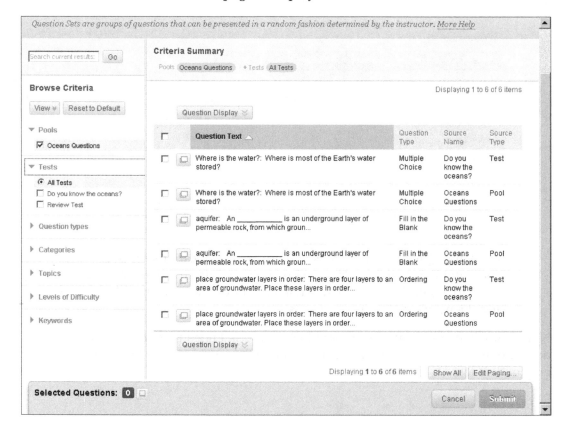

2. Select the pools and tests from which you want to select the questions.

3. After selecting at least one pool or test, you can use the other search criteria. This is optional.

4. The results of your search are listed on the right-hand side of the page. Select the questions that you want to include in the random block.

5. Click on the **Submit** button. You are returned to the **Test Canvas** page. **Question Set** is displayed on this page:

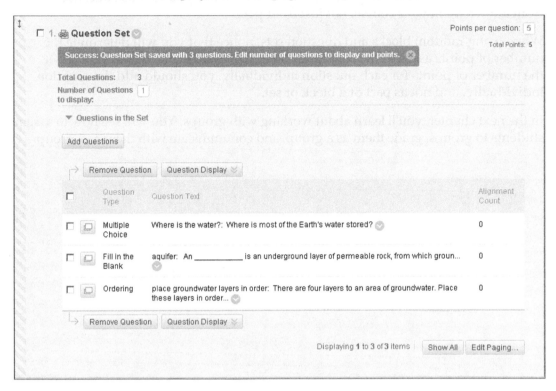

6. The **Total Questions:** field tells you how many questions are there in the block. The **Total Points:** field tells you how many points all the questions are worth, taken together. You can change the number of questions the block displays, and the number of points per question.

Note that when you create a random block, you don't need to give it a name or description. This is because the block will not exist outside of the test. It exists only on this test.

Summary

Question pools are the key to making groups of questions that can be reused. Random blocks give you an easy way of limiting the display of questions on a test to just a selected pool or pools. Question sets enable you to reuse questions from anywhere in your course, not just from pools.

When using random blocks and question sets, notice that you will determine the number of points assigned to each question in the block or set. If you want to set the number of points for each question individually, you should add the question individually, and not as part of a block or set.

In the next chapter, you'll learn about working with groups. You will see how to assign students to groups, grade them as a group, and communicate with them as a group.

8
Working with Groups

Blackboard enables you to place the students of a course into groups. When you group students, you gain some capabilities and get some limitations. You can use groups to organize the students who are in a course into teams, and also to separate students into different classes, while they use the same Blackboard course.

In this chapter, you will be learning the following topics:

- Creating groups
- Assigning students to groups
- Enabling students to choose their own groups
- Setting up the group setting for an activity
- Sending e-mails to all the members of a group

Some group activities are visible to everyone in the course. But only the members of the specified group can edit the activity. When a group activity is visible to everyone, but only group members can participate, it's as if everyone in the class can "watch" the group perform the activity.

Some group activities are visible only to members of the specified group. In this case, groups cannot see each other's work in the activity.

The visibility of a group activity is a default setting. It can be changed to allow or prevent people from outside the group to see the group's activity.

Like other activities, a group activity can be graded. When you give a grade for a group activity, everyone in the specified group gets the same grade. Once you enable the grading for a group activity, you cannot reverse that setting.

As of this writing, you can create a maximum of 99 groups per course. This is a limit of the system, and not a limit set by the site administrator.

Creating groups

Blackboard enables you to create groups one at a time, and to create several groups at once. In Blackboard, creating several groups at once is called **batch create**. Also, you can automatically enroll the students in the group(s) randomly or manually, or allow students to enroll themselves. A student can be a member of several groups at once.

Creating a single group with manual enrollment

The following procedure is the most basic—to create one group and manually enroll students into it:

1. From the **Course Management** menu on the left menu bar, select **Users and Groups | Groups**.

2. Select **Create Single Group | Manual Enroll**. The **Create Group** page is displayed:

> There is no notification when a student manually enrolls into a group that you have created. You will need to check the progress of enrollment by opening the group.

3. The **Name** and **Description** fields will be visible to the members of this group. You should use the **Description** field to inform students about the purpose of the group.

4. The options under **Tool Availability** determine which tools are available to the members of this group.

5. Your Blackboard installation might be configured to give each group certain tools, such as its own blog, forum, and group e-mail list:

   ° If you enable the setting for **Blogs**, then the group gets a blog. Each member of a group can create entries for the group's blog. All course members, including those not in the group, can read and comment on entries made in the group blog, but cannot create new entries.

   ° If you enable the setting for **Discussion Board**, then group members can create and manage their own forums, which are exclusive to the group.

- ° If you enable the setting for **Email**, then group members can e-mail individual members or the entire group.

- ° If you enable the setting for **File Exchange**, then the group members and the teacher can exchange files in an area set aside just for this group. All members can add and delete files.

- ° When you add a group for **Journal**, all members of the group can view entries made by the other members. Students outside the group cannot see the group's journal.

- ° If you enable the setting for **Tasks**, then group members can create tasks that are assigned to the group as a whole. Any group member can complete a group task.

- ° If you enable the setting for **Wikis**, then the group gets a wiki. Each member of a group can create entries for the group's wiki. All course members, including those not in the group, can read entries made in the group wiki, but cannot create new entries.

6. Under the **Membership** section, select the students you want to put into this group:

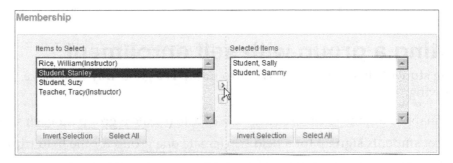

7. Save it by clicking on the **Submit** button.

The **Groups** page displays the group that you just created:

Creating a group with self enrollment

Allowing students to enroll themselves in a group is a good way to achieve the following:

- Enable students to choose sides in a debate (create a group for each side)
- Let students sign up for a field trip (create one group for the field trip)
- Encourage students to form study groups (create several groups and let the students sort out the membership, times, and locations)

The following procedure shows you how to create the group, and what it looks like from the student's point of view, when the student joins the group:

1. From the **Course Management** menu on the left menu bar, select **Users and Groups | Groups**.

2. Select **Create Single Group | Self-Enroll**. The **Create Group** page is displayed.

3. The **Name** and **Description** fields will be visible to members of this group. You should use the **Description** field to inform the students about the purpose of the group.

4. The options under **Tool Availability** determine which tools are available to the members of this group:

    ° If you enable the setting for **Blogs**, then the group gets a blog. Each member of a group can create entries for the group's blog. All course members, including those not in the group, can read and comment on entries made in the group blog, but cannot create new entries.

    ° If you enable the setting for **Discussion Board**, then group members can create and manage their own forums, which are exclusive to the group.

    ° If you enable the setting for **Email**, then group members can e-mail individual members or the entire group.

    ° If you enable the setting for **File Exchange**, then the group members and the teacher can exchange files in an area set aside just for this group. All members can add and delete files.

    ° When you add a group for **Journal**, all members of the group can view entries made by the other members. Students outside the group cannot see the group's journal.

    ° If you enable the setting for **Tasks**, then group members can create tasks that are assigned to the group as a whole. Any group member can complete a group task.

    ° If you enable the setting for **Wikis**, then the group gets a wiki. Each member of a group can create entries for the group's wiki. All course members, including those not in the group, can read entries made in the group wiki, but cannot create new entries.

5. Under the **Sign-Up Options** section, enter a name and instructions for the sign-up sheet. The students will see these when they sign up for the group.

6. Also under the **Sign-Up Options** section, the **Show Members** setting will enable students to see other students who have chosen the same group. This is useful when you want them to organize themselves into teams.

7. Save it by clicking on the **Submit** button.

The **Groups** page displays the group that you just created:

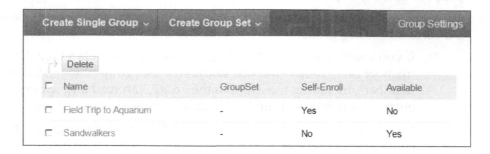

Create Single Group ⌄	Create Group Set ⌄			Group Settings
□ Delete				
□ Name	GroupSet	Self-Enroll	Available	
□ Field Trip to Aquarium	-	Yes	No	
□ Sandwalkers	-	No	Yes	

Now, let's add a link to the Course Menu so the student can see this group:

8. From **Course Menu**, select **Add Menu Item | Tool Link**.

9. From the **Type** drop-down list, select **Groups**.

10. Enter the **Name** field for the link.

11. Select the **Available** checkbox.

12. Click on the **Submit** button.

A link to the **Groups** page is added to the **Course Menu**. This will enable the students to get to the groups that you create for them:

From the student's point of view—self-enrollment into a group

Now that the self-enrollment group is created, let's look at it from the student's point of view. The following instructions are written for the student:

1. From **Course Menu**, select the **Groups** link. The **Groups** page is displayed:

Field Trip to Aquarium

To sign up for the field trip to the aquarium, join this group.

Date and Time: January 3, 2013. We will leave the school at 8:30am sharp and return to school by 2:30pm.

Cost: no charge.

 Sign Up

Sandwalkers

The members of this group will complete assignments that focus on life on the beach, above the surf line.

---

2. Notice that the student has two groups listed on this page. The **Sandwalkers** group was assigned by the teacher. The **Field Trip to Aquarium** group requires that the student sign up.

3. Click on the **Sign Up** button. The **Sign Up Sheet** page is displayed:

Sign Up Sheet

SignUp Sheet Name : Sign Up for Field Trip to Aquarium

SignUp Sheet Instructions : Sign up here for the field trip! This sign-up sheet is the only way we know if you're coming on the trip.

Field Trip to Aquarium

To sign up for the field trip to the aquarium, join this group.

Date and Time: January 3, 2013. We will leave the school at 8:30am sharp and return to school by 2:30pm.

Cost: no charge.

Group Members : Sammy Student, Suzy Student
Sign Up

In the previous screenshot, the **SignUp Sheet Instructions:** group and its description are displayed. This was entered when the teacher created the group.

4. Click on the **Sign Up** button.

5. The student is enrolled into the group, and taken back to the **Groups** page:

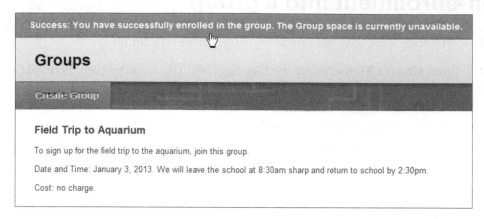

Notice that at the top of the page in the previous screenshot, the student sees a **Success:** message. A part of this message tells the student that **The Group space is currently unavailable**. This is because when the instructor was creating this group, under **1. Group Information**, the instructor chose to make this a sign-up sheet only:

Because of this setting, all of the group tools (Blog, Journal, Wiki, Email, and so on) are unavailable. The instructor can always change this setting. For example, perhaps after the field trip, the instructor will make the group available to the students, and ask them to write in the group wiki about the trip.

Consider using the Announcements and/or Messages feature to tell your students that they need to sign up for a group.

Creating multiple groups at once

The feature that you use to create multiple groups at once is called **group sets**. When you create a group set, you will specify whether to use self, manual, or random enrollment. We have already seen how self and manual enrollments work. Let's create a group set using random enrollment:

1. From the **Course Management** menu on the left menu bar, select **Users and Groups | Groups**.

2. Select **Create Group Set | Random Enroll**:

You can also create group sets with self enrollment and manual enrollment. Because we have already created groups with these kinds of enrollments, we are going to use random enrollment in these instructions.

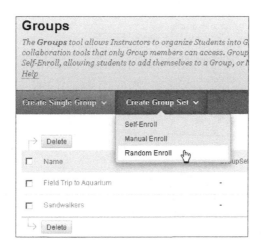

The **Create Random Enrollment Group Set** page is displayed.

3. Just like when you create a single group, you will enter a name and description for the group. However, be aware that Blackboard is going to create several groups with the name that you enter, and it will add a number to the end of the name. Make sure that the **Name** field you enter will still make sense when Blackboard adds a number to the end of it:

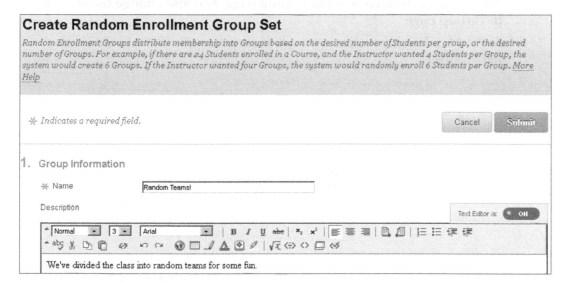

4. Under **2. Tool Availability**, you will choose which tools are available to each group. Note that each group in the set will get its own copy of each tool that you select:

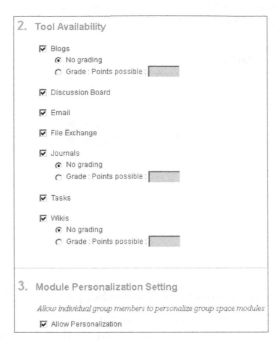

5. If you select **Allow Personalization**, individuals in the group will be able to customize the group space by adding personal modules such as What's New, change the layout of their group page, and also change the style of the group page.

6. In the **Membership** section, you will first choose how Blackboard creates the groups:

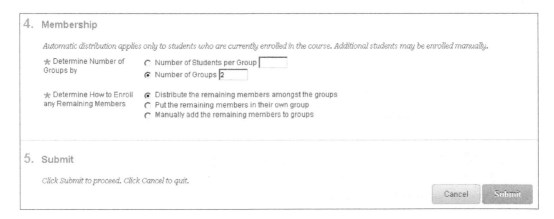

If you select **Number of Students per Group**, Blackboard will put the number of students that you specify into each group. It will create as many groups as needed, to place every student into a group. Each group will have at least as many students as you specify. If there are students left over after creating the groups, the next setting will determine how to handle the extra students. For example, if you have 20 students, and you select three students per group, Blackboard will create six groups of three students. This will use 18 of the students. There will be two students left over.

If you select **Number of Groups**, Blackboard will create the number of groups that you specify, and then divide the students as evenly as possible among these groups. If the number of students cannot be divided exactly by the number of groups, there will be students left over. The next setting will determine how to handle the extra students. For example, if you have 20 students and you select six groups, Blackboard will create six groups of three students each. This will use 18 of the students. There will be 2 students left over.

7. Also under **Membership**, you will specify what Blackboard will do with the extra students who are left after creating the groups.

8. Click on the **Submit** button to create the groups.

Blackboard will create the groups, name them, and return you to the **Groups** page:

Notice that Blackboard added a number to the end of each group's name.

After you use the **GroupSet** feature to create multiple groups, you can always open a group and edit its membership manually. In the following screenshot, the instructor is editing the membership of the group **Random Teams! 1**, which was created in the previous procedure:

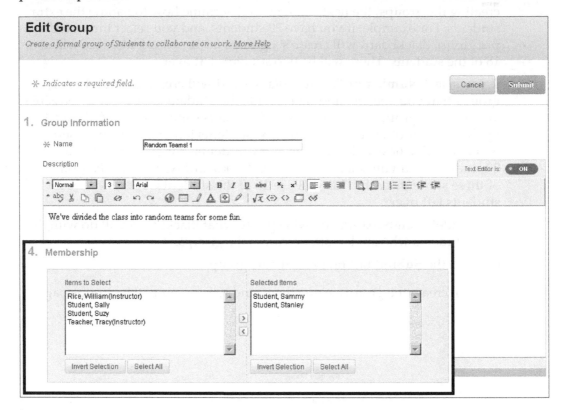

How group settings affect activities

At the beginning of this chapter, we said that applying a group to different kinds of activities has different effects on those who can participate in, and see the activities. When you create a group, Blackboard creates a number of tools for that group, by default. In the following screenshot, you can see the **Sandwalkers** group page, and the tools that Blackboard automatically added to this group:

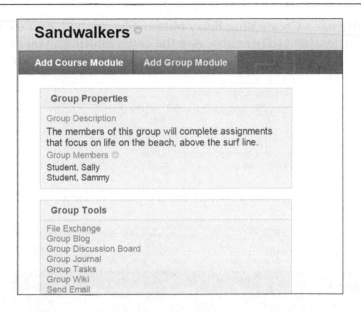

The exact tools available to a group depend upon how your Blackboard system is configured.

Note that Sally is a member of this group. Let's look at the group blog from a member's and non-member's point of view. First, here is the group blog from Sally's point of view:

Notice that **Sally** has a **Create Blog Entry** button. She can both create entries, and comment on entries. Next to her entry, **Are the crabs molting?**, you can see an icon for a pull-down menu, which enables the student to edit her own blog entry:

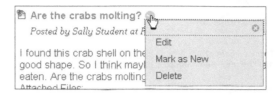

Now, let's look at the blog from a non-member's point of view:

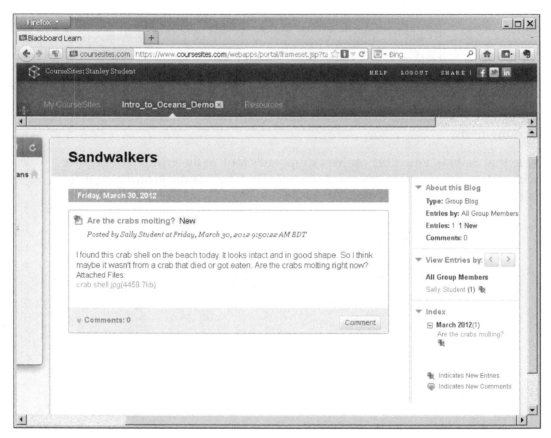

Note that the non-member does not have a **Create Blog Entry** button, so (s)he cannot add entries to the blog. However, there is a **Comment** button, which enables the non-member to add comments to an entry.

As you can see, group blogs are open to non-members. So if you want a writing activity, which is open only to group members and closed to all others, you would need to override this default setting and deliberately close the blog to non-members. Also, while members can get to a group blog through the **Groups** page, non-members will not have that group on their **Groups** page. So for a non-member to access another group's blog, that non-member would need to go through the **Blogs** tool link on the Course Menu.

The following table lists group tools, and tells you who can participate and see these tools. This can help you choose the right tool for your situation:

Activity	When used with a group...		What effect does a group have on grading?
	who can see it?	who can edit or submit it?	
Assignment	Only the members of the group.	Any member of the group.	All members get the same grade.
File Exchange	Only the members of the group.	Any member of the group can submit, download, and delete any file in the group area.	Not applicable. If you're grading students on files that they submit, use Assignment instead.
Blog	All members of the course, even those not in the group.	Only members of the group can post entries to the blog. Everyone in the course can comment on the posts.	All members get the same grade.
Discussion Board	Only the members of the group can see the group's Discussion Board.	Only the members of the group can contribute to the group's Discussion Board.	Posts can be graded. As the posts are made by individual group members, the individual, and not the group, receives the grade.
Journal	Only the members of the group can see the group's Journal.	Only the members of the group can contribute to the group's Journal.	All members get the same grade.

Activity	When used with a group...		What effect does a group have on grading?
	who can see it?	who can edit or submit it?	
Wiki	All members of the course, even those not in the group. However, non-members cannot edit group wiki entries. They can comment on the entries.	Only members of the group can edit a wiki. The following screenshot shows a member's view of the wiki. Notice the buttons for **Edit Wiki Content** and **My Contribution**.	All members get the same grade.

Tasks	Only the members of the group can see the group's Tasks.	Any member of the group can mark any Task as not started, in progress, or completed, as shown in the following screenshot.	Not graded.

Sending e-mails to members of a group

The teacher can always use the groups **Email** tool to send an e-mail to the members of a group. The teacher finds this tool by selecting **Groups** from the main menu, and then clicking on the drop-down menu icon next to the name of the group:

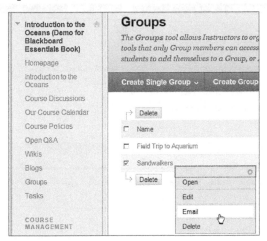

Students can send e-mails to members of their group only if the teacher has enabled the **Group Email** tool for them. To enable this tool for your students, perform the following steps:

1. From the **Groups** page, next to the name of the group, select the drop-down menu icon:

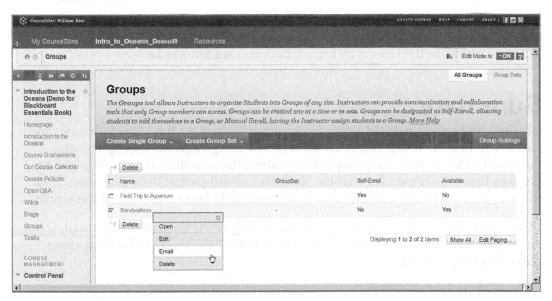

2. In the drop-down menu, select **Email**. The group's e-mail page is displayed:

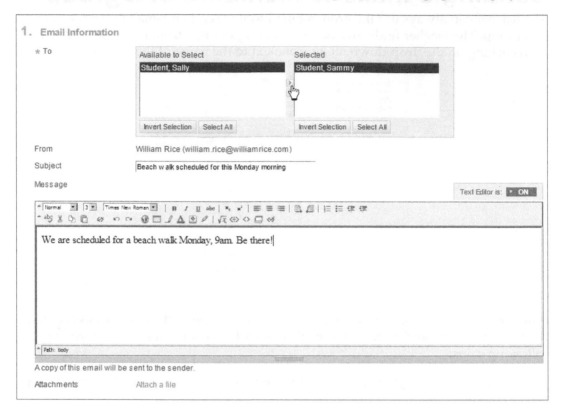

3. Fill out the **Email** fields, and click on **Submit** to send your message.

This tool works in the same way for teachers and students alike.

Summary

Groups can be used to build a camaraderie, teach students how to collaborate, and encourage healthy competition. To successfully use groups for these purposes, you need to know how the group settings affect the activities. Even as you use the **Groups** function, remember that the students are still part of the whole class, and most of their activities and interactions will probably be as members of the whole.

In the next chapter, we'll focus on communicating with students using Email, Announcements, and Messages. You will see how these tools can be used along with the group settings.

Communicating with Students Using E-mails, Messages, and Announcements

Blackboard gives you several options for communicating with your students, as follows:

- E-mails
- Messages
- Announcements

Each of these has a place in your workflow and can fulfill different purposes. This chapter will help you understand these options, and show you how and when to use each method.

In this chapter you will learn how to:

- Send an e-mail to the external e-mail addresses of your students
- Send an internal Blackboard message to the students in your course
- Post an announcement on your students' home page

The difference between e-mails, messages, announcements, and alerts

When you send an e-mail to your students from within a Blackboard course, the e-mail is sent to the e-mail address that is in the student's profile. While the e-mail is sent from Blackboard, it comes from the e-mail address that is in your profile.

When you send a message to your students, the message is sent from your Blackboard account, to their Blackboard accounts. They must log in to Blackboard to read the message.

An announcement is not automatically sent to a student in the way that an e-mail or message is sent. As an option, you can choose to have the system send an announcement to the recipients via e-mail. Announcements appear on the student's home page, in a section for announcements. Of course, the student must log in to see them. You can set a time limit for an announcement. That is, you can tell it to appear and disappear on specific dates and at specific times.

Alerts are automatically generated by Blackboard when you set a deadline for coursework. For example, if you set a deadline for an assignment, Blackboard will automatically generate an alert as the deadline approaches. Alerts appear on the student's home page, in a section for alerts.

Sending an e-mail to your students

Blackboard allows you to send an e-mail to your entire class, any student who is a member of a group, only selected groups, or only selected individuals. To send an e-mail from Blackboard, perform the following steps:

1. From the main menu on the left-hand side of the screen, select **Course Tools**.

2. Select **Send Email**.

3. Select the type of recipient:

Send Email

Instructors can send email to all or selected individual Users, Students, Groups, Teaching Assistants, Instructors or Observers. From a Blackboard Learn course, email cannot be sent to anyone who is not a member of the course.

All Users
Send email to all of the users in the Course.

All Groups
Send email to all of the Groups in the Course.

All Teaching Assistant Users
Send email to all of the Teaching Assistant users in the Course.

All Student Users
Send email to all of the Student users in the Course.

All Instructor Users
Send email to all of the Instructor users in the Course.

Single / Select Users
Select which users will receive the email.

Single / Select Groups
Select which Groups will receive the email.

---

4. Select recipient(s) and enter the details of the e-mail, as shown in the following screenshot:

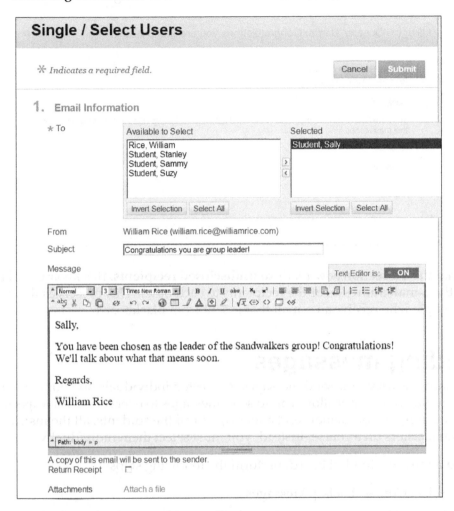

5. Click on the **Submit** button to send the e-mail.

6. The recipient will receive an e-mail, which shows the e-mail address of the sender in the **From** section, as shown in the following screenshot:

Note that the **To** section now reads **to undisclosed recipients**. Blackboard will not reveal the e-mail addresses of the recipients to each other. This preserves the privacy of the people who receive an e-mail that is sent from Blackboard.

Sending messages

Blackboard allows you to send messages to selected individuals on your course. Unlike e-mail, it does not allow you to send messages to everyone with a specific role. For example, you cannot send a message to all the students, all the instructors, or all the teachers on a course. Instead, you must select them individually.

To send a message in Blackboard, perform the following steps:

1. Select **Course Tools | Messages**.
2. On the **Messages** page, click on the **Create Message** button. The **Compose Message** page is displayed, as shown in the following screenshot:

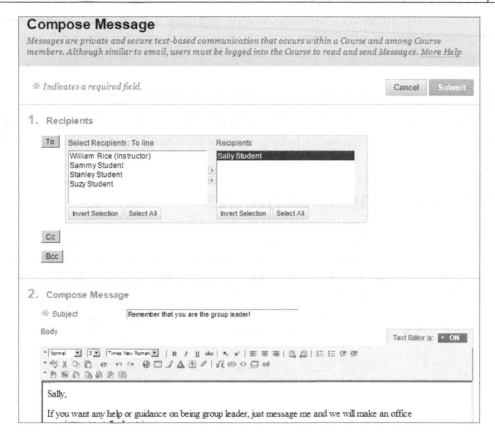

3. To select recipients, click on the **To**, **Cc**, and/or **Bcc** buttons, and select their names.

4. Enter the subject and body of your message in the **Subject** and **Body** sections, respectively.

5. Click on the **Submit** button to send your message.

The **Messages** page shows you the **Inbox** and **Sent** folders. Unlike the **Email** page, the **Messages** page gives you an easy way to see the communication that you have had with class members.

> The **Messages** page is different for each course. Messages that you have sent and received in one course, will not show up on the **Messages** page of any other course that you are in.

However, when composing a message, you do not have the option of selecting an entire group of people, or all those with a specific role in your course (such as all the instructors or all the students). Sending an e-mail gives you these choices.

Keep backups of your student communications!

Blackboard does not keep a backup or archive of sent messages or e-mails. If student contact is audited or in any way needed for reference, remember to keep copies of the e-mails in another system.

Posting announcements

By default, announcements appear on a student's home page. Announcements can be accessed from several places on the page. In this example, you can see that the **Announcements** tool is available under the **Student Tools** menu. Announcements are also available in the **What's New** block, where the **Announcements** block is displayed, as shown in the following screenshot:

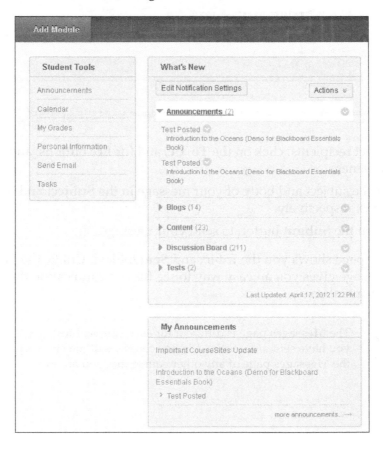

Once the student is inside our demonstration course, he/she will notice that the course also has an **Announcements** block on the course's **Homepage**, as shown in the following screenshot:

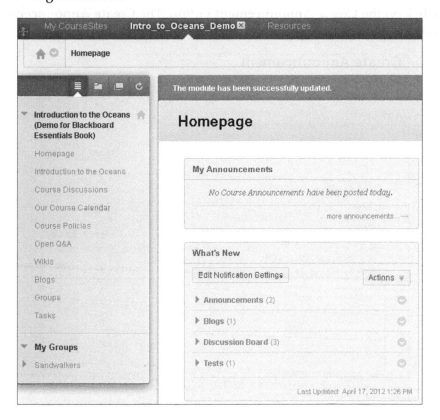

Why you should add the Announcements block to your course's home page

In the preceding screenshot of the student's home page, there are three places where the student can access announcements. However, don't rely on this! That's because the student's home page can be edited by him/her. So the student could remove these tools from his/her home page. In the immediately preceding screenshot of the course's **Homepage** page, the **My Announcements** and **What's New** blocks cannot be removed by the students. They were placed there by the teacher, so you can rely on them being displayed when the student enters the course.

To send an announcement to your students, perform the following steps:

1. Select **Course Tools | Announcements**.

2. Click on the **Create Announcement** button. The **Create Announcement** page is displayed, as shown in the following screenshot:

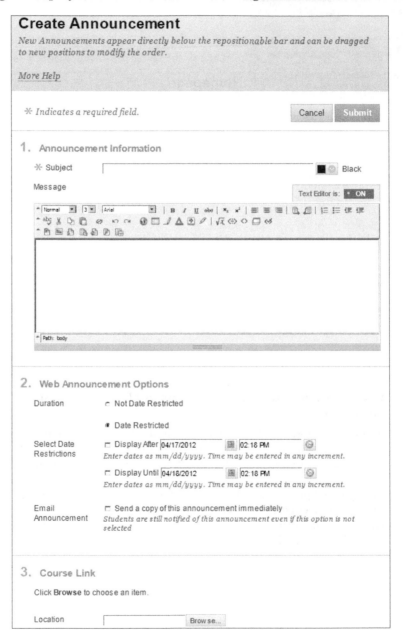

3. Note that there is no place to select recipients for the announcement. The announcement that you create here will be displayed to all the course members.

4. In the **Announcement Information** section, enter the content of your announcement.

5. You can use **Duration** and select the **Date Restricted** option to display the announcement for a selected period of time. Outside of this time period, course members will not be able to see the announcement. The teacher, however, will be able to see all the announcements that were sent in this course.

6. Your Blackboard system might be configured to send an e-mail to the members of a course when an announcement is posted. Check with your system administrator. Some users might choose to suppress these e-mails. If they do, selecting **Email Announcement** will override their choice and send an e-mail to the students even if they have chosen to suppress them.

7. If your system is configured to send an e-mail when an announcement is posted, that e-mail will be sent immediately. This happens even if the announcement's date and time are restricted.

8. To post the announcement, click on the **Submit** button.

Summary

One of the key differences between messages and e-mails is the student's ability to see the history of their communication about a course. When you send an e-mail from Blackboard, that e-mail is sent to a student's e-mail account. This e-mail now exists outside of Blackboard. Even if the student is no longer enrolled in the course or if the course is closed, the student can refer back to his/her personal e-mail archive. When you send a message using Blackboard's message feature, the message exists only in that course. If the student is no longer enrolled in the course or if the course is closed, the student will not be able to retrieve the message. This can be a factor when deciding whether to use e-mail, or messages, to communicate with your students.

Announcements are useful when you want a message to have an expiration date. You can use them to remind students of upcoming events and deadlines.

In the next chapter, you will learn how to use Blackboard Collaborate to conduct live, web-based sessions with your students.

10
Using Collaborate/ CourseSites Live

Collaborate is Blackboard's application for holding live, web-based sessions with your students. Collaborate is a separate product from their **Learning Management System (LMS)** application, which is Blackboard Learn. Until now, this book has dealt only with the Blackboard LMS.

If your company has purchased Blackboard Learn, they might also have purchased Collaborate. You should check with your system administrator.

If you are using Blackboard's free site for educators — coursesites.com, Collaborate is part of their offering. On coursesites.com, Collaborate is labeled as **CourseSites Live**.

If your company has purchased Blackboard Learn, but not Collaborate, you can just open a free account on coursesites.com and use the **CourseSites Live** tool. You will need to recreate your students' accounts on coursesites.com, as it is a totally separate system from your company's LMS. But being able to hold online meetings might be worth the extra work for you.

Blackboard maintains detailed user guides for Collaborate. This chapter cannot take the place of those detailed guides. However, the pages in this chapter will get you started with using Collaborate's essential features.

For example, the September 2011 edition of *Blackboard Collaborate Web Conferencing Moderator's Guide* is over 330 pages long. It is organized by feature, so if you have a specific feature that you want to learn about, it is relatively easy to find that feature.

This chapter is about one-tenth as long, so it cannot contain nearly as much detail. In addition to being much shorter, this chapter is organized chronologically. It takes you through the process of hosting a basic Collaborate session, from start to finish. For example, it's not until page 106 that the official Blackboard guide says, "Generally speaking, it is recommended that you configure your audio before the session begins". We will deal with configuring your audio in the *Configuring audio and video* section.

If you have access to two computers side by side, you can play the part of the teacher and a student, and follow along on your own computers. For example, you might want to try this if your institution has a computer lab.

During our demonstration session, we will show you how to:

- Make Collaborate available to your students
- Configure audio and video settings
- Share a PowerPoint slideshow
- Use whiteboard tools
- Use the chat feature
- Talk over audio
- Take your students on a web tour
- Share an application

Making your first online meeting a test session

Consider making your first online meeting a test session. During this session, you and your students will practice with the software. Before the session, you can send an agenda to your students, telling them exactly what will happen during the session, and what to do if they get lost or if Collaborate doesn't run properly for them. A sample agenda might look as follows:

Our CourseSites Live Test Session

When we will meet: August 14, 2012, at 3 p.m. EST.

Where we will meet: From your home computer.

What you will need: Your computer, a built-in microphone or microphone that you can plug in, and at least a DSL or cable modem.

Who will meet: All of us! This is a compulsory activity.

How we will meet: Using the **CourseSites Live** tool.

At least two days BEFORE the test session (on August 11 or 12)

Using the same computer and browser (which you will use for our meeting), go to the following link (you should be able to just click it):

```
http://support.blackboardcollaborate.com/ics/support/
default.asp?deptID=8336&task=knowledge&questionID=1473.
```

This will bring you to a page where you can automatically test your setup to ensure it is compatible with Collaborate.

If there are any problems with the software, send a Blackboard Message to the teacher immediately!

DURING our test session

If you lose audio, use the chat feature to tell me. I will help you to troubleshoot.

Each student (including you!) will take turns to speak.

I will share a document with the class.

Each student will take turns to use the "whiteboarding" features to mark up the document.

I will send a poll question to the class. Everyone will respond.

And more!

AFTER our test session

If you had any problems during the test session and we did not get to solve them, send a message to me. We can schedule the time for another session.

Making Collaborate available to you and your students

The Collaborate tool is always available to you, the teacher, under the **Course Tools** submenu. Adding it to **Course Menu** will make it available to your students and make it faster for you to access it. Perform the following steps:

1. From the **Add Menu Item** list, select **Create Tool Link**.
2. From the drop-down list where you select the tool that you want to add, select either **CourseSite Live** or **Collaborate**.
3. Enter the name for the collaboration tool.
4. Set the tool's availability.
5. Click on the **Submit** button. A link for the tool is added to **Course Menu**.

Launching the Collaborate tool

The first time that you or a student launch the Collaborate tool, you will be prompted to download and install the software. Perform the following steps:

1. From **Course Menu**, select the **Collaborate** tool.
2. Blackboard displays a launch page for the collaborate tool. If you've never launched it, the page displays a **Launch** button. If it has been launched before, it displays a **Re-launch** button. Click on the button.
3. Blackboard might prompt you to select your internet speed (**Dial-up**, **DSL/Cable**, and so on). If so, select one and continue.
4. Blackboard Collaborate will be launched in a new window or in a new tab, depending on your browser.
5. Collaborate is a Java application. If your browser launches Java automatically, Collaborate will run without prompting you. If your browser is configured to send a prompt before running Java applications, you will see a prompt like the following screenshot:

6. Click on **OK** in the dialog box to launch Collaborate. Blackboard will display a message telling you not to close the browser window until Collaborate has finished being launched. Then, Collaborate will be launched in its own window, as shown in the following screenshot:

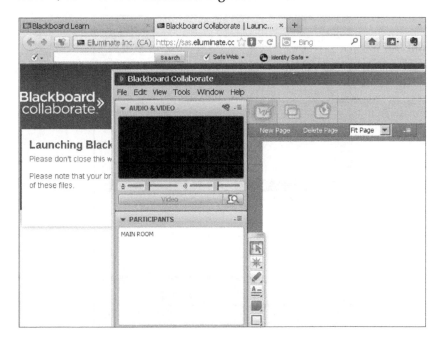

You're ready to test your microphone and speakers.

Configuring audio and video

Definitely before you start your first session, and preferably before each session, you should configure your audio and video settings to ensure that they work. Perform the following steps:

1. From the **Audio & Video** panel, select the **Start the audio setup wizard** icon, as shown in the following screenshot:

2. **Audio Setup Wizard** is launched in a new window. On a Windows or Linux computer, the next step will require you to select an input device:

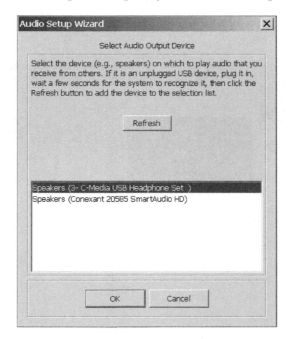

If your computer has only one input device, such as the built-in microphone in most laptops, only one will be displayed.

3. Select the input device and click on the **OK** button. The wizard will guide you to set the volume levels for your microphone and your speakers.

Showing a PowerPoint slideshow

If you want to show a PowerPoint slideshow, you have two options. First, you can use screen sharing; that is, you can run the slideshow in PowerPoint, while sharing your screen with the class. If you and your students have enough bandwidth, this will give you all the transitions and effects that you would get if you were showing the slideshow in person.

Your second option is to bring that PowerPoint slideshow into Collaborate, and let Collaborate convert and display it. Collaborate will convert each of your slides into a page, in a Collaborate whiteboard. The bad news is, the special effects and animations will be lost. The good news is, you and the students can mark up your slideshow using the whiteboard tools, as you discuss the presentation.

To bring a PowerPoint slideshow into Collaborate, perform the following steps:

1. Create your slideshow in PowerPoint. Save it, and close PowerPoint. When Collaborate converts the slideshow to its own format, it will require PowerPoint to be closed.

2. Select **File | Open | Whiteboard**. The **Load File** dialog box is displayed, as shown in the following screenshot:

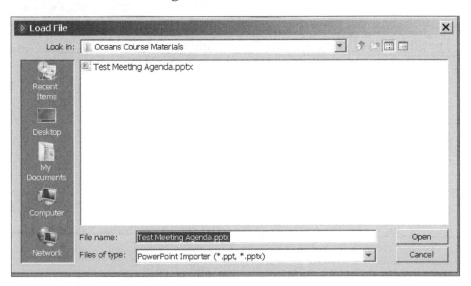

Notice that the **Files of type:** field checks for the PowerPoint files (***.ppt** and ***.pptx**), by default.

3. Navigate to the directory where your slideshow is saved.

4. Select the slideshow and click on the **Open** button. You will see messages indicating that the slideshow is being converted:

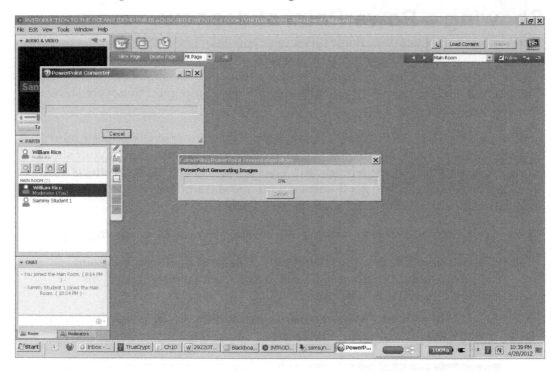

5. The slideshow is displayed in Collaborate's main window:

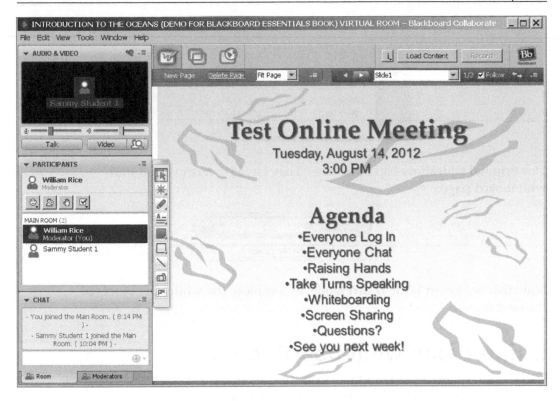

Let's explore some features on this page.

Notice that we are in Whiteboard mode. You have two visual clues. The **Whiteboard** icon is highlighted, as shown in the following screenshot:

And, from the **View** menu, **Whiteboard** is selected:

Our original slideshow had two slides. They have been converted into whiteboard pages:

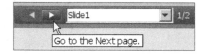

Now that we are in Whiteboard mode, let's explore the whiteboard tools in the next section.

Using basic whiteboard tools

Collaborate's whiteboard offers an extensive list of tools. Let's look at the most basic, which you will use in most of your whiteboard sessions.

You already saw the previous and next buttons, which you use to go to different pages in your whiteboard:

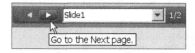

To the right-hand side of these buttons, you will see the **Show Page Explorer** icon, as shown in the following screenshot:

The page explorer shows you a thumbnail view of each page in the whiteboard. These pages are shown under the **Main Room** section, as shown in the following screenshot:

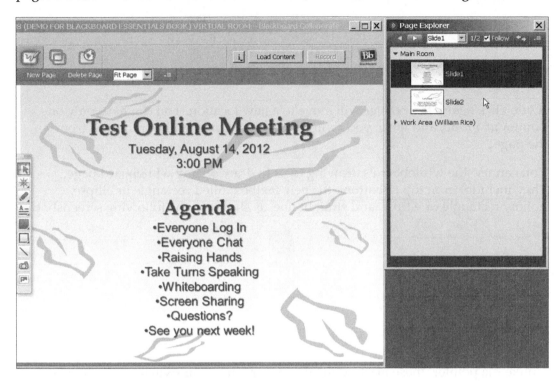

To show a page, double-click on its thumbnail image.

 To rearrange the pages in your whiteboard, just drag-and-drop them in the page explorer.

To point out an item of interest, use one of the pointers from the toolbox:

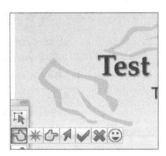

When you click on any of the available pointers, the pointer will stay stuck where it was, as shown in the following screenshot:

If you click again, the pointer will move to a new location. You can have only one pointer at a time, and when you switch tools, the pointer will be removed from the page.

You can use the whiteboard's drawing tools to draw on any whiteboard page. They include, from top to bottom, the pen, textbox, filled rectangle or ellipse, hollow rectangle or ellipse, and straight line, as shown in the following screenshot:

Unlike the pointer, these marks don't disappear when you switch tools or pages. They remain until you select and delete them.

To select an object which you have placed on a whiteboard page, use the select tool from the top of the toolbox:

When an object is selected, you can resize, move, or delete it.

There are other whiteboard tools, but these are the most basic.

Using the chat

Collaborate includes a basic chat feature. In the following screenshot, you can see that the teacher (the "moderator") has the option of having a chat with either the entire class or just the other moderators in the session:

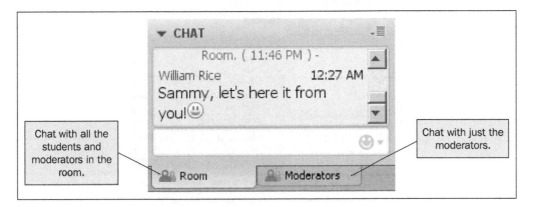

Any chat message that the student sends is, by default, shown to the entire class:

The teacher can start a private chat between a student and the teacher. In the **PARTICIPANTS** panel, right-click on a student's name. From the pop-up menu, select **Send a Private Chat**, as shown in the following screenshot:

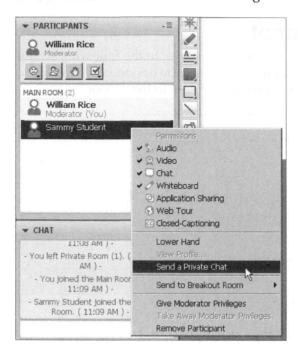

The student can also start a private chat with the teacher or another student in the same way, by right-clicking on the teacher's or the student's name.

Why use a private chat?

Private chats can be useful when you want to do the following:

- Help a student who is having trouble with his/her audio or video
- Discreetly tell a student that their question or comment is not appropriate
- Give extra help or encouragement to a student, whom you know is having trouble with the topic
- Acknowledge an emoticon that the student has posted (more on emoticons in the next section)

You can save the transcript of a chat as a text file. Select **File | Save | Chat...**, and choose the location and filename of the text file.

Using emoticons during a Collaborate session

When you are sending a text message to a friend, emoticons are those cute little faces that you add to the message to show your mood, for example 😊. When you are teaching an online class, emoticons serve a more serious purpose. They take the place of the facial expressions and body language that you would get in a face-to-face class.

Collaborate allows the students to indicate their mood by selecting an emoticon from the list in the **PARTICIPANTS** panel. The following is a screenshot of **Suzy Student 1** indicating that she is confused at this point in the session:

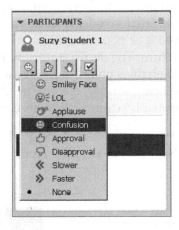

The moderator and the other students will see the emoticon next to her name in the **PARTICIPANTS** panel, as shown in the following screenshot:

Emoticons are displayed for a few seconds, and then they disappear.

Emoticons are not just silly, smiley faces!

Encourage your students to use emoticons to communicate how they are feeling about the course. Make using them part of your practice session. Emoticons are no more inappropriate or intrusive than the facial expressions that we see in every face-to-face class.

Talking in Collaborate

There are two ways to talk in Collaborate. If your company has purchased the telephony feature, then you can use a telephone conference to talk with your students while having a Collaborate session. If you don't have the telephony feature (because your company hasn't purchased it or you are using `Coursesites.com`), you can use Collaborate's built-in audio feature. The audio feature works with your computer's microphone and speakers, and enables you to converse with your students. You don't need a telephone conferencing service. All you need is Collaborate, and the microphone/speakers that (probably) came with your computer.

In a previous section of this chapter, we went through the testing of our audio using **Audio Setup Wizard**. Now let's look at the **Audio & Video** panel:

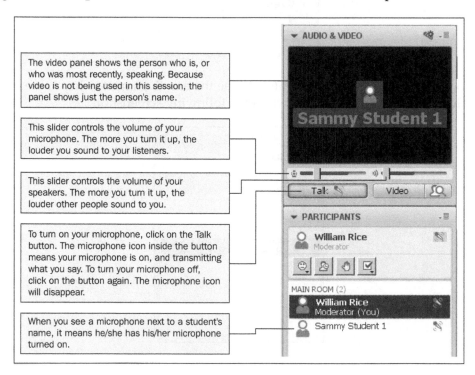

To speak to your students, just click on the **Talk** button and start speaking. If everyone has gone through **Audio Setup Wizard**, they will hear what you are saying.

If a student leaves his/her microphone on, and you want to turn it off for him/her, right-click on the student's name and select **Audio** to remove the check mark from that ability. That will turn off their microphone:

Doing this will completely remove the ability for the student to use audio. To immediately restore the student's ability to use audio, right-click on the student's name again and select **Audio**. The student's microphone will still be off, but the student will be able to use it again.

Collaborate allows multiple people to speak at the same time. You can select the maximum number of simultaneous speakers. If anyone in the session has very limited bandwidth, you might need to limit the number of speakers. To do this, from the **Audio and Video Options** menu, select **Maximum Simultaneous Talkers...**, as shown in the following screenshot:

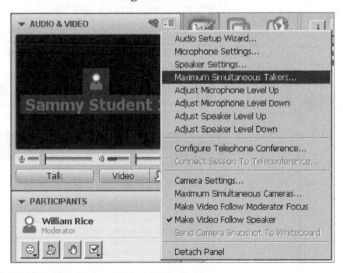

Audio is especially important when you are sharing your screen with your students, for example, to discuss the contents of the whiteboard, or a web tour or application that you are sharing.

Taking your students on a web tour

Using the Web Tour feature, you can share web pages with your students. To begin a web tour, perform the following steps:

1. Click on the **Web Tour** icon, as shown in the following screenshot:

2. Enter the URL (web address) of a page that you want to show your students into the address field.

3. Press *Enter*.

The web page will be displayed in the main area of the students' Collaborate window, as shown in the following screenshot:

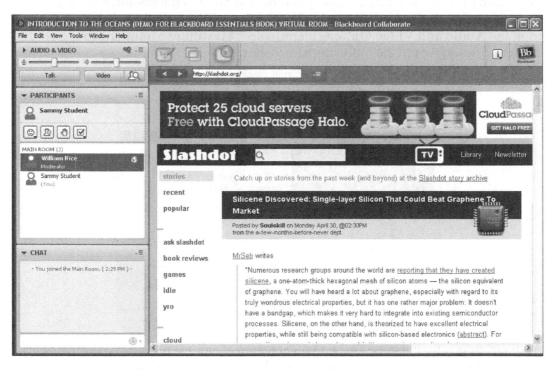

During a web tour, every time you go to a new page you can make your students follow you to the new page. That happens when the **Follow Me** checkbox is selected, as shown in the following screenshot:

After you lead the students to a web page, the students can travel to other web pages. But every time that you go to a new page, the students are taken there with you.

Dropping your students on a web page with Web Push

During a web tour, your students usually follow you to each new web page that you display. And, the web pages are displayed in Collaborate's main window. With Web Push, you will launch your students' default browser and open a web page of your choice for them. If Web Tour is like a journey that you take together, Web Push is like dropping your students off at a destination. After that, they are on their own.

To send a web push to your students, perform the following steps:

1. Click on the **Web Tour** icon, as shown in the following screenshot:

2. From the **Options** menu next to the URL field, select **Open URL in Browser...**, as shown in the following screenshot:

3. At the prompt, enter the web address of the page you want to open, and then click on the **OK** button.

 A web push can be a good way to end a Collaborate session. You can drop the students off on a web page with links and information, which encourages them to explore the topic further.

Sharing an application on your computer

Application sharing enables the teacher and students to share an application or their entire desktop with the participants. The shared application is displayed in Collaborate's main window. As the teacher, you can:

- Share an application or your entire desktop with the class
- Give and take back control of the application/desktop that you are sharing, to a student
- Give and take back the ability to share an application/desktop to a student

During a practice session with your students, you might want to practice each of these. You might also want to have students practice scaling the application so that it fits on their displays.

 I recommend against sharing your entire desktop, unless you have a good reason to show everything. Students might have trouble fitting your desktop on their screens, and it's too easy to accidentally show a document name, stray folder, or other items that you don't want to share.

To share an application, perform the following steps:

1. Open the application that you want to share. Resize its window so that it will fit on your students' screens with room around it.

2. In Collaborate, click the **Application Sharing** button. A list of the open applications is displayed:

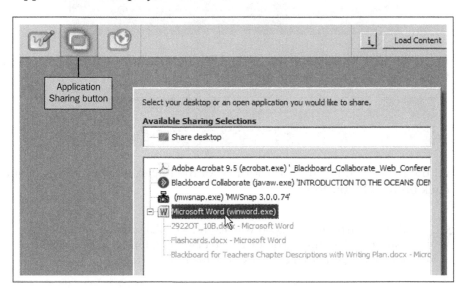

Note that while **Microsoft Word** has three open documents in the application list, you must select the entire application. You cannot select just one of its windows.

3. Select the application and click on the **Share** button. A yellow frame will appear around the application that you select. You are now sharing this application.

In the example shown in the following screenshot, you can see that the teacher has selected to share Microsoft Word. Word has several documents open. The yellow frame is around all of the documents:

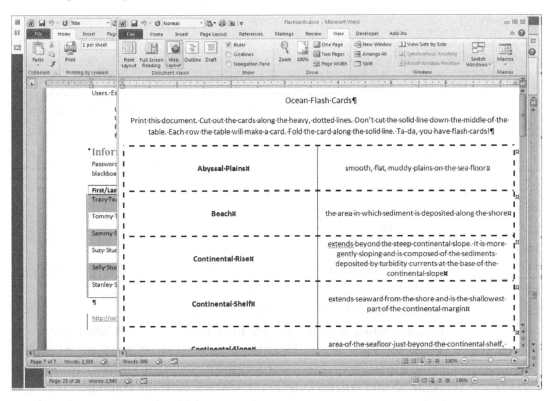

The student is seeing all of these shared windows, inside the student's Collaborate window, as shown in the following screenshot:

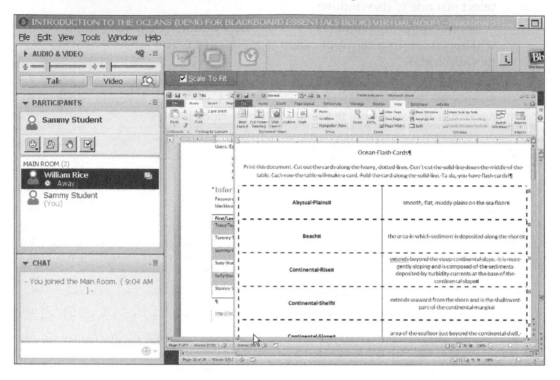

4. If your students cannot see all that you are sharing, they can do three things to see more of the application. The students can:

   a. Maximize the size of their Collaborate application.

   b. Deselect **Show Side Bar** to hide the panels on the left-hand side, under the **View** menu. This makes more room for the main window.

   c. Clear the check mark from the **Scale To Fit** checkbox. The application being shared will no longer be resized to fit in the student's Collaborate main window. Instead, it will be shown at its original size, even if all of it doesn't fit. The student might need to scroll around the screen.

5. If the application that you are sharing has several windows open and if you want to show just one of the windows, close or minimize the ones you don't want to share. The yellow sharing frame will shrink to surround just the window that you have left open.

Compare the following screenshot of one open window with the preceding screenshot that showed several windows open:

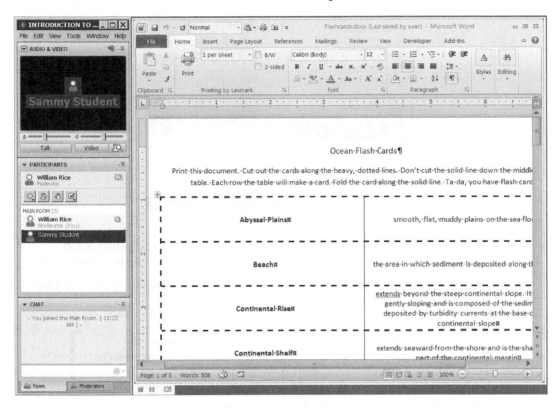

Giving a student the ability to share an application

As the moderator of a Collaborate session, you can give the ability to share an application to any of the participants. To give sharing privileges to a student, perform the following steps:

1. First, you must stop sharing your own application. If you are still sharing an application, your application sharing privileges will override any sharing privileges that you give to the student.

2. Next to the student's name, select **Application Sharing**, as shown in the following screenshot:

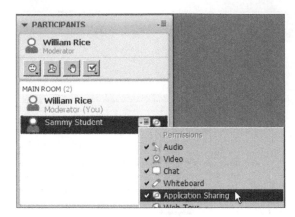

At this point, you have given the student that ability to do application sharing. But now the student must perform several steps to begin sharing.

3. The student selects the **Application Sharing** icon. A list of the applications to be shared is displayed.

 If the **Application Sharing** icon is not selectable, the student should select a different mode and then reselect the **Application Sharing** icon.

4. From the list, the student selects the application to be shared.

5. At any time, the teacher can remove the student's ability to share, by right-clicking the student's name again, and removing the check mark from **Application Sharing**.

Whiteboarding over a shared application

I must confess that the title of this section is not entirely honest. You can't use whiteboard tools to draw on top of a shared application! However, the ability to mark up and comment on a shared application is so useful that I will propose a workaround for you.

While sharing the application that you want to whiteboard on, click on the **Screenshot** icon on the yellow frame:

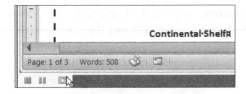

Blackboard will take a screenshot of the window, bring you back to the Collaborate application, and place that screenshot on a whiteboard. In the example shown in the following screenshot, you can see that we are in the whiteboard mode and the whiteboard tools are available:

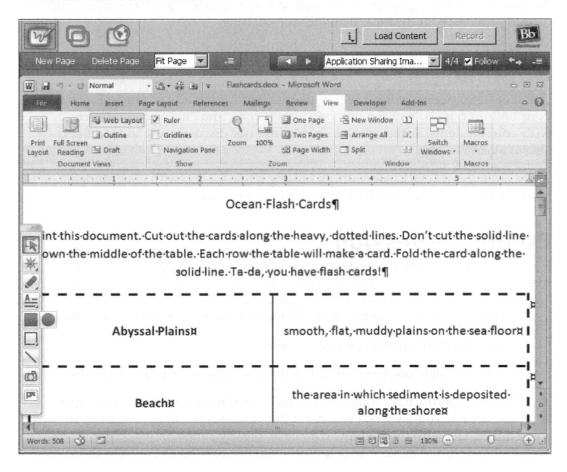

Now you can mark up the screenshot like any other whiteboard page.

When you are ready to resume application sharing, click on the **Application Sharing** icon and select **Resume Sharing**, as shown in the following screenshot:

If you want to save the marked-up whiteboard page for your students to refer to, select **File | Save | Whiteboard**. You can save it as a whiteboard file, a PDF document, or a PNG graphic. This is a good way to create a quick reference guide or study guide about the topic that you were sharing.

Summary

Collaborate (or **CourseSites Live**) is an excellent way to add a human touch to your online courses. You can use voice, emoticons, and chat to communicate with your students. Although this chapter did not discuss using video, that is also available to you.

There are several keys to successfully hosting a live session with your students. Many of them were implied in the previous instructions.

Before the session

Have your students test their systems first. Blackboard provides a free site where they can do this: `http://support.blackboardcollaborate.com/ics/support/default.asp?deptID=8336&task=knowledge&questionID=1473`. Make this testing, and reporting to you that they did the test, an assignment in your course.

Make your first online meeting a practice session.

Have a welcome slide displayed so that students see it as soon as they enter the session.

If you're using audio, have some kind of audio greeting for students when they enter the session, so they won't wonder if their audio is working. You can play some music, talk with the students who have already joined, or just keep watch over the session, and make sure you greet everyone as soon as they join the session.

During the session

Encourage students to use emoticons to communicate how they are feeling about the session.

Design your slideshows, shared applications, and other presentation material to fit inside the Collaborate's main window. Yes, it's true that students can maximize the window and even completely hide the sidebar. Most of them won't. And some of your students might have small displays (such as a netbook). Plan for it.

Let students use whiteboard tools to illustrate and clarify things during your discussion. Then, save one or more whiteboard pages as PDF or PNG files. They will make good reminders of your discussion.

After the session

At the end of the session, consider using Web Push to drop your students off on a web page that provides the starting point for their next actions.

After the session, use Blackboard's message or e-mail feature to send the students screenshots of the session, a summary, next steps, and any other follow-up information. Explicitly tell them what they learned and what is expected from them.

And most of all, have fun with the online session! It's a chance for you to step out from behind the online course, and interact with your students in a more personal way.

11
Grading Students

Blackboard's Grade Center is a spreadsheet that shows the students' grades, and calculations based on those grades. Only a user with the role of Instructor, Teaching Assistant, or Grader can access Grade Center.

In this chapter, we will show you how to:

- Find things that need to be graded
- Use Smart Views to view the gradebook
- Categorize graded items
- Manually override grades
- Prepare a report for grades

When a student wants to see his/her grades, the student selects the **My Grades** tool, and not **Grade Center**.

Blackboard automatically enters the grades for graded activities such as tests, assignments, graded posts in forums, and so on. Each graded activity gets a column in **Grade Center**. Each student gets a row in **Grade Center**. In the following screenshot, you can see that there are columns for graded activities, such as **Where did you**, **Water Walks**, and more. There is also a row for each student:

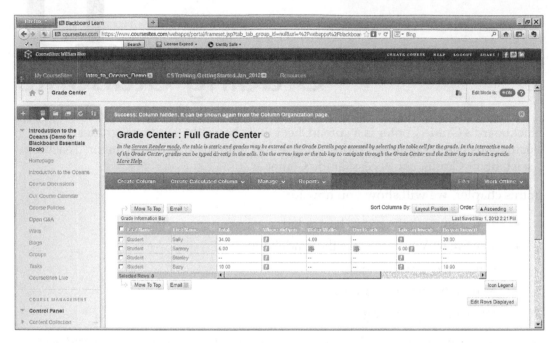

Notice the column labeled **Total**. This is a calculated column. Calculated columns can give you the total, average, and minimum/maximum for a group of selected grade columns.

While Blackboard adds a grade column for each graded activity in the course, you can also add your own grade columns. This would be useful if you were grading an activity or item that Blackboard has not added to **Grade Center**. For example, you might grade students on class participation. Class participation is not a Blackboard assignment, test, or other online activity. So if you want to grade it, you would need to add a column for it to the gradebook. You could also do this to grade attendance for a field trip.

Viewing Grade Center

To view **Grade Center**, from the **Course Management** menu, select **Grade Center**. In the following screenshot, the user has then selected **Full Grade Center**:

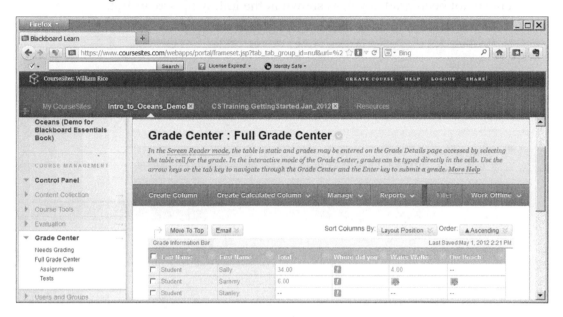

In the menu on the left-hand side, note that under **Full Grade Center**, there are two more options—**Assignments** and **Tests**. These are Smart Views that were chosen by the user as favorites. They can also be set by the Blackboard administrator, and/or created by the user. We will discuss more about Smart Views later.

In a later section of this chapter, we will focus on how to customize your view of **Grade Center**.

Finding things that need to be graded

To see a list of the things that need grading, just select **Grade Center | Needs Grading**. **Grade Center** will display a list of the graded activities in your course, which have not been graded yet, as shown in the following screenshot:

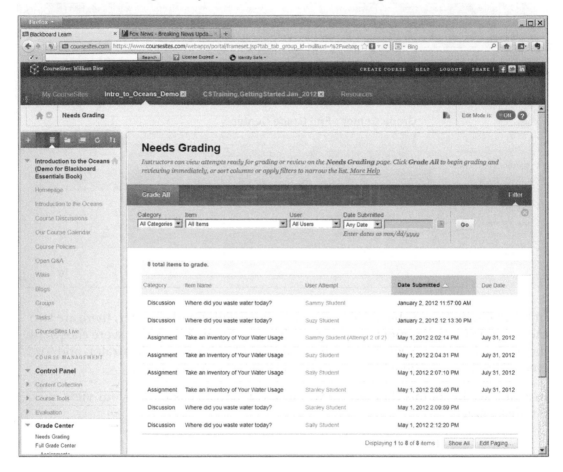

You can sort the items by clicking on any column heading. Most useful might be **Due Date**, so you can grade the items that were recently due and make sure you have graded everything in a timely manner. You can also sort by the items by name. For example, you may be in the mood to grade a particular assignment; you can use the filter accordingly, to see only what you need.

One important limitation of the **Needs Grading** display is that only graded activities, which Blackboard automatically adds to the gradebook, appear in this display. That is, it shows only those items for which the student has submitted something in your course.

If you add a graded activity for which nothing is done in Blackboard, it will not appear here. For example, in **Full Grade Center**, shown in the following screenshot, you can see that students are graded on their attitude. This is a column that the teacher manually added to **Grade Center**. Attitude is not a Blackboard activity. Therefore, it does not appear in the **Needs Grading** display, shown in the preceding screenshot.

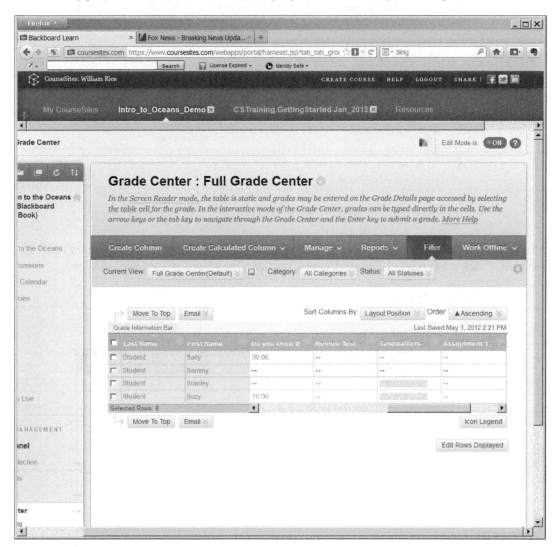

If you have added grade columns to **Grade Center**, don't depend on the **Needs Grading** display to tell you if those columns need to be graded. Instead, look for them in **Full Grade Center**.

We'll see how to enter grades in a later section.

Smart Views

Under the **Current View** drop-down menu, you will find a list of Smart Views under the **Smart Views** submenu, as shown in the following screenshot:

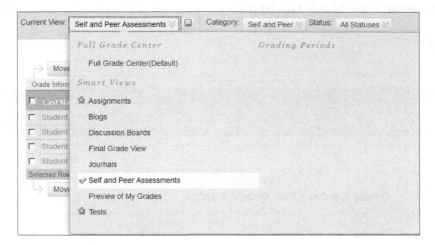

Smart View is a search condition. Blackboard comes with some Smart Views built in for you. Under **Manage | Smart Views**, you can build your own Smart View:

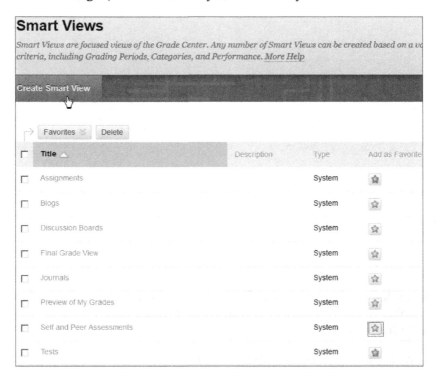

Notice that **Assignments** and **Tests** are designated as favorites. That is why they appear under the **Full Grade Center** submenu, as shown in the following screenshot:

When you create your own Smart View, you will select the columns and search criteria that you want. I suggest that you become adept at creating new columns and filtering views before you try to create a new Smart View. Until then, experiment with the ones provided by Blackboard.

Creating Grading Periods

Note that, by default, there are no **Grading Periods** in your course:

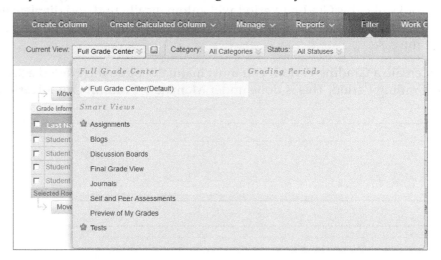

A Grading Period displays all of the grades that are due during a specific time period. In this example, we are creating a Grading Period that will display all those activities that are due to be graded in May:

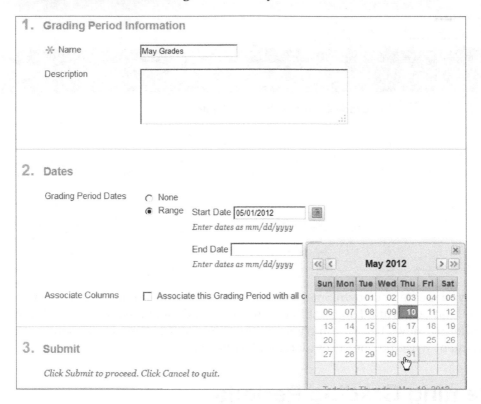

When we choose **Grading Period Dates**, it looks like we are creating a search criteria. That is, it looks like this Grading Period will automatically find and display all of those activities that are due to be graded between May 1 and May 31, 2012. However, this is not the case.

After you create a Grading Period, you must manually place the graded activities into that Grading Period. This is done under **Manage | Column Organization**:

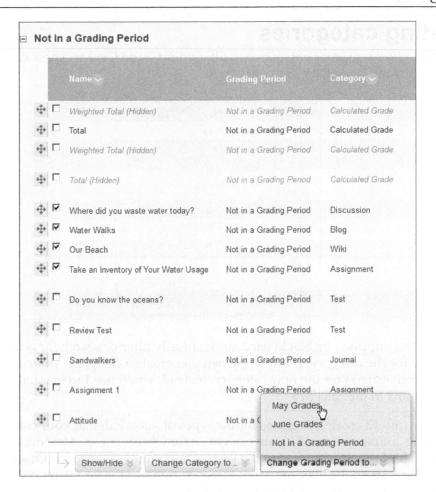

As the teacher, you will need to ensure that the due dates that you display to the students, and the dates for the Grading Period match each other.

> You cannot create Grading Periods with overlapping dates. For example, we cannot create a Grading Period for May, and another for June, and then another for May and June.

Creating categories

Blackboard gives you some categories to filter your **Grade Center**. These categories represent the kind of activities in your course:

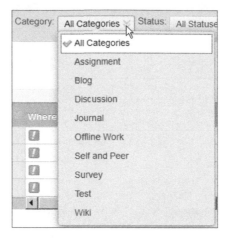

The categories supplied by Blackboard automatically filter or search for activities that qualify for the category. However, when you create a category, you cannot create a search criteria for the new category. Instead, you'll need to manually assign columns to the category.

You might want to create categories for the types of knowledge in your course. In our example course, we could create categories for Observations, Memorization, and Analytical Thinking. We can assign the journal and wiki grades to the Observations category, our tests to the Memorization category, and grades for forum posts and assignments to the Analytical Thinking category.

You can create a new category under **Manage | Categories**. You can add a column into a category under **Manage | Column Organization**.

Smart Views, Grading Periods, Categories...this is getting confusing!

Smart Views, Statuses, and Categories are all independent filters. They work together to allow you to filter and see only the grade columns that you need. For a column to be shown, it must meet the criteria set by all of these. Grading Periods work by themselves. If you select a Grading Period, you cannot use **Category** or **Status** to filter the display.

If all this filtering is still confusing you, just switch between **Full Grade Center** and the filters that you are trying to understand. This will show you, by example, the effects that each filter has on the display of grades.

Showing, hiding, and moving rows

Just like you can move and hide rows in a spreadsheet, you can manipulate the display of rows in **Full Grade Center**. Note that you cannot do this in the **Needs Grading** window. You must be in **Full Grade Center** to move and hide rows.

To move a row or rows to the top of the page, click the checkbox at the beginning of the row(s) and then click on the **Move To Top** button, as shown in the following screenshot:

To hide rows or show rows that were hidden, use **Manage | Row Visibility**. To sort by a column, click on the column name.

Some examples of filtering and finding

Let's look at some examples of using the filters in **Grade Center**. First, here is an example of the teacher displaying all the students who have not attempted **Review Test** yet. To do this, the teacher has selected **Status** as **Not Attempted** and **Current View** as **Tests**, as shown in the following screenshot:

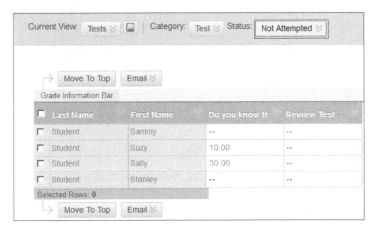

Note that even though **Suzy** and **Sally** took one test, they did not take the second test. Therefore, their rows also appear when we search for tests that have not been attempted.

In this example, the teacher is displaying the Grading Period of **May Grades**. Notice that when displaying a Grading Period, the choices for **Category** and **Status** are not available:

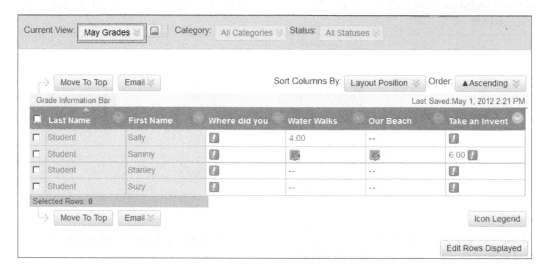

In this example, the teacher has selected **Status** as **Needs Grading**. That is the only filter that the teacher is using:

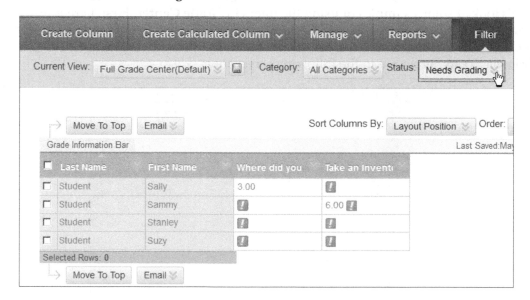

Assigning and entering grades

Now that you can find the items you want in **Grade Center**, it's time to give them grades. In general, there are two ways to give an item a grade. You can open the item, which will take you deeper into **Grade Center** where you will view just the item that you are grading. You would do this if you needed to examine the item before giving a grade. Or, you can enter a grade right into **Grade Center**. You would do this if you already knew the grade that you wanted to give.

Screen Reader Mode

In the following screenshot, **Grade Center** is in **Screen Reader Mode**. In this mode, you cannot enter grades directly into **Grade Center**. This is a fast way to locate items that you know need to be graded, and enter grades for them. You must select the item and select **View Grade Details** for that item, as shown in the following screenshot:

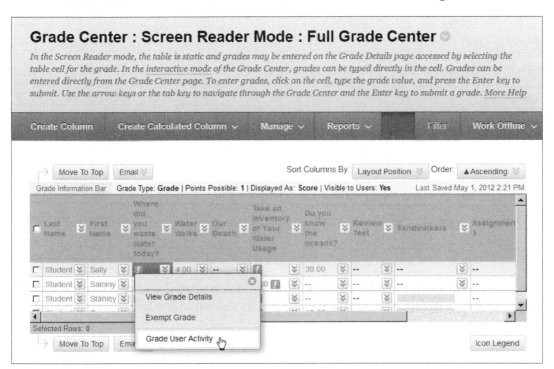

The **Grade Details** page looks slightly different for each kind of activity. However, its features and functions are consistent. In this example we will see the **Grade Details** page for a graded forum entry, as shown in the following screenshot:

The teacher clicks on the **Edit Grade** button and is presented with a pop-up window where he/she can enter the grade and details, as shown in the following screenshot:

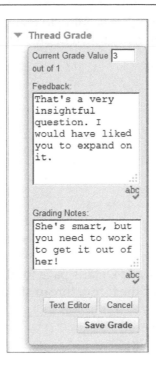

The **Feedback** field is visible to the student. The **Grading Notes** field is visible only to teachers and graders.

Manually overriding an automated grade

In the preceding example, the activity was manually graded. That is, the teacher had to look at the student's work to grade it. Some activities do not require manual grading. For example, a test that has only automatically graded questions doesn't require the teacher to assign a grade.

Even though Blackboard calculates a grade for some activities, such as tests, you can manually override the grade. Begin by selecting **View Grade Details** from the pop-up menu next to the item.

In the following example, the teacher is going to manually override a grade for a test called **Do you know the oceans?**, as shown in the following screenshot:

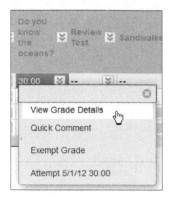

This brings the teacher to the **Grade Details** page for that test. It looks a little different from the **Grade Details** page for the forum thread shown in the previous example:

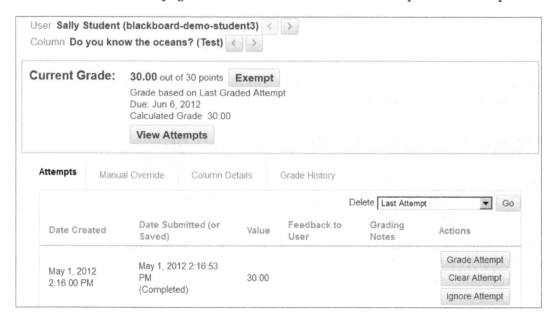

Clicking on the **Manual Override** link displays a screen where the teacher can enter a new grade, leave feedback for the student, and enter a grading note for the teacher(s):

In the preceding screenshot, notice the **Grade History** link on the right-hand side. When you override a calculated grade, it will be recorded under the item's grade history.

Entering all of the students' grades for an activity

If you want to grade all of the students who completed an activity, you can do this from a single page. From one page you will view a student's work, grade it, and move on to the next student who completed that activity.

In **Grade Center**, from the drop-down menu in the activity's column, select **Grade Attempts**, as shown in the following screenshot:

Some activities won't have **Grade Attempts** available in their drop-down menu. If that is the case, then open the drop-down menu next to a specific student's attempt and select **Grade User Activity**, as shown in the following screenshot:

In both cases, you will be taken to a page that displays the first student's attempt at the activity:

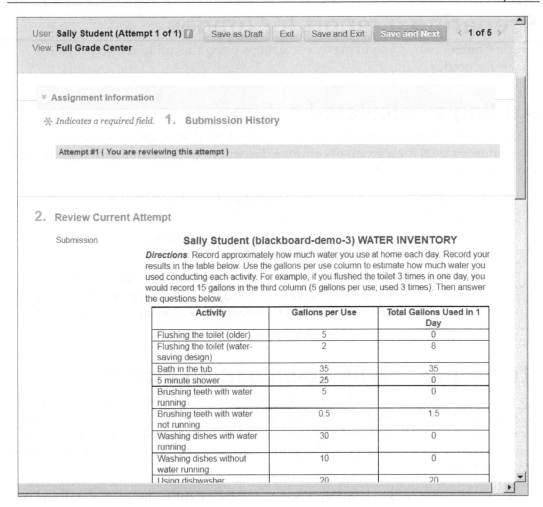

Note that the buttons at the top of the page show you which student's work you are grading. They also enable you to move to the next and previous students.

The rest of the page shows the same information as if you were viewing the grade detail page for a single student. This is the fastest way to grade an assignment for all the students in your class.

Preparing a report for grades

Grade Center enables you to make calculations using the grade and to prepare a report for grades.

Adding a calculated column

A calculated column can display the average, weighted average, minimum/maximum, or total for a group of columns. To determine which columns are used in the calculation, perform the following steps:

1. To create a calculated column, select **Create Calculate Column** from the menu bar in **Grade Center**. You will then select the type of calculation you want.

2. On the **Create Column** page, you select the columns to use in the calculation. You will also select other settings on this page.

3. After you create a column, it is added to the rightmost position in **Grade Center**. You will probably need to scroll to the right to find it. You might want to use **Manage | Column Organization** to reposition the column that you created.

Reporting versus downloading grades

The **Reports** menu option enables you to create and print reports that show data from **Grade Center**. If you have the ability to print PDF or XPS files, you can create a report for each student and e-mail that report to them. However, a limitation of the Report feature is that it creates only printed reports. You can read the data, but you cannot do anything with it.

If you want to analyze grade information, you might want to import it into Excel or another spreadsheet program. Looking at **Grade Center**, there is no "export" function apparent. However, under the **Work Offline** menu, there is a **Download** option. This option enables you to download all, or part of **Grade Center** to a text file. If your computer has Excel installed, it will probably offer to open that file in Excel as you download it.

Summary

Blackboard's Grade Center offers you a lot of functionality from just one place. You can search, organize, enter, calculate, and report on grades from the **Full Grade Center** page. Use the Filters and Smart Views to ensure that you are viewing only the data you want. Use Grading Periods and categories to organize your grades. The **Grade Attempts** and **Grade User Activity** options will save you time by enabling you to grade all of the students' attempts at an activity, on one page. With so much information available in one place, it can be easy to lose sight of the big picture. This is especially true because Grade Center cannot be made to fill your entire monitor. Occasionally, you might want to download your entire gradebook to a spreadsheet and look at it in full screen mode, or even print it out on multiple sheets and look at it all at once. In general, Grade Center can be a good way to see where you are in the progress of the course, what has been done, what the students are attempting, and what needs to be done.

Index

A

activities
  group settings, effects 164-168
  students' grades, entering for 226, 227
alerts 172
announcements
  about 7, 8, 172, 176
  posting 176, 177
  sending, to students 178, 179
Answer Formula 133
application
  sharing, on computer 201, 202
application sharing
  ability, for students 203, 204
assignment
  about 22, 23, 109
  creating 110-112
  responding to 113-118
automated grade
  manually, overriding 223, 224

B

batch create 154
Blackboard
  about 27, 121, 153, 171, 209
  announcements, posting 176, 177
  announcements, sending
        to students 178, 179
  blank test, creating 122
  categories, creating 218
  course home page 6, 7
  e-mail, sending to students 172-174
  e-mails, sending to group members 169, 170
  groups, creating 154

  messages, sending to students 174-176
  questions, creating 125
  tests, creating 121
  video file, uploading 20
Blackboard, features
  announcements 7, 8
  assignment 22, 23
  blog 16
  content page 12-14
  discussion board 8
  forum 17, 18
  gradebook 10-12
  groups 24, 25
  learning module 14, 15
  video 19, 20
  wiki 21
Blank Page
  about 30
  adding, to Content Area 33, 34
  adding, to course 31-33
Blank Page tool 30
Blank question 136
blank test
  creating 122
blog
  about 16, 167
  grading 100-104
  link, creating to 98-100
  managing 100
blog comments
  deleting 104, 105
  editing 104, 105
blog entry
  deleting 104, 105
  editing 104, 105

C

calculated column
 adding, in Grade Center 228
calculated formula question 131-135
calculated numeric question 135
categories
 creating 218
Collaborate
 application sharing, for students 203, 204
 application, sharing on computer 201, 202
 whiteboarding, over shared application 204-206
computer
 application, sharing on 201, 202
content
 adding, to Content Area 30
Content Area
 about 27, 28
 adding, steps 28, 29
 Blank Page, adding 33, 34
 content, adding 30
 hiding 29
 image, adding to 70
 Learning Module, adding 37-42
Content Collections 51
Content Page 12-14
Correct/Incorrect question 136
course
 Blank Page, adding 31-33
 image, adding to 69
 video, adding to 56
Course Asset
 link, adding to 69
Course Menu
 Course Tools, adding 47, 48
course page
 test, adding to 123
Course Tools
 about 44
 adding, to Course Menu 47, 48
 adding, to Home Page 48
Create Tool Link 46

D

Discussion Board
 about 8, 167
 link, creating to forum 84, 85
downloading grades
 versus reporting 228

E

Either/Or question 136
e-mail
 about 171
 sending, to group members 169, 170
 sending, to students 172-174
essay question 136

F

file
 adding 52-54
 adding, for download 50
 versus item 50
File Response question 136
filters
 using, in Grade Center 219, 220
forum
 about 17, 18
 link, creating to 84, 85
 managing 86
 posts, collecting 86-89
 posts, grading 90, 91
Full Grade Center
 rows, displaying 219
 rows, hiding 219
 rows, moving 219

G

Gradebook 10-12
Grade Center
 about 209, 210
 calculated column, creating 228
 filters, using 219, 220

grades, assigning 221
grades, entering 221
grading list, searching 212, 213
reporting, on grades 228
Screen Reader Mode 221-223
Smart Views 214, 215
viewing 211
graded activities
placing, into Grading Period 216, 217
grades
assigning, in Grade Center 221
entering, in Grade Center 221
reporting on 228
Grading Periods
about 215
creating 216
dates, selecting 216
graded activities, placing into 216, 217
group
about 24, 25
creating 154
creating, with manual enrollment 154, 155
creating, with self enrollment 156-158
group activities 153
group members
e-mails, sending to 169, 170
group sets 160
group settings
affects, on activities 164-168

H

Home Page
Course Tool, adding 48
home page, BlackBoard 6, 7
Hot Spot question 137, 138
HTML editor
used, for composing page 34-36

I

image
adding, to Content Area 70
adding, to course 69
item
adding 54-56
versus file 50

J

Journal activity 167
Jumbled Sentence question 138

L

Learning Module
about 14, 15, 37
adding, to Content Area 37-42
learning path 37
Likert question 139
link
adding, to Course Asset 69
adding, to Wikis page 107, 108
creating, to blog 98-100
creating, to forum 84, 85

M

manual enrollment
single group, creating with 154, 155
Matching question 139
messages
about 172
sending, to students 174-176
Multiple Answer question 139
Multiple Blank question 136
Multiple Choice question 139
multiple groups
creating, at once 160-163
My Grades tool 10, 209

O

Opinion Scale question 139
Ordering question 140

P

page
composing, with HTML editor 34-36
posts
collecting, in forums 86-89
grading, in forum 90, 91

Q

question behavior
  determining, with Question Settings page 122, 123
question pool
  about 141, 144
  creating 144-147
questions
  adding, on Test Canvas 123
  answer feedback, adding 127-129
  answers, adding 127-129
  categories, adding 129, 130
  creating 125
  creating, on Test Canvas 123
  keywords, adding 129, 130
  notes, adding 129, 130
question sets
  about 142, 150
  creating 150, 151
  versus random blocks 140-144
Question Settings
  used, for determining question behavior 122, 123
Question Settings page 122
question text 126, 127
question title 126, 127
question types
  about 126-130
  Blank 136
  calculated formula 131-135
  calculated numeric 135
  Correct/Incorrect 136
  Either/Or 136
  essay 136
  File Response 136
  Hot Spot 137, 138
  Jumbled Sentence 138
  Likert 139
  Matching 139
  Multiple Answer 139
  Multiple Blank 136
  Multiple Choice 139
  Opinion Scale 139
  Ordering 140
  Quiz Bowl 140
  Right/Wrong 136
  Short Answer 140
  True/False 136
  Yes/No 136
Quiz Bowl questions 140

R

random blocks
  about 142-144
  creating 148, 149
  versus question sets 140-144
reporting
  versus downloading grades 228
Right/Wrong question 136
rows
  displaying, in Grade Center 219
  hiding, in Grade Center 219
  moving, in Grade Center 219

S

Screen Reader Mode, Grade Center 221-223
self-enrollment
  group, creating with 156-158
  viewing, from student's view 159, 160
Short Answer question 140
single group
  creating, with manual enrollment 154, 155
Smart Views, Grade Center 214, 215
static course material 49
students
  announcements, sending to 178, 179
  e-mail, sending to 172-174
  messages, sending to 174-176
students' grades
  entering, for activity 226, 227

T

tasks 168
test
  about 23
  adding, to course page 123
  creating 121
Test Canvas
  questions, adding on 123
  questions, creating on 123

Test Canvas page
about 125
navigating to 125
Test Options page
about 124
implementing 124
True/False question 136

U

uploaded files, in course 18, 19

V

video
about 19, 20
adding, to course 56
video file
uploading, into BlackBoard 20
Vimeo 19

W

whiteboarding
over shared application 204-206
wiki
about 21, 106, 168
creating 106, 107
Wikis page
link, adding to 107, 108

Y

Yes/No question 136
YouTube 19

About Packt Publishing

Packt, pronounced 'packed', published its first book "*Mastering phpMyAdmin for Effective MySQL Management*" in April 2004 and subsequently continued to specialize in publishing highly focused books on specific technologies and solutions.

Our books and publications share the experiences of your fellow IT professionals in adapting and customizing today's systems, applications, and frameworks. Our solution based books give you the knowledge and power to customize the software and technologies you're using to get the job done. Packt books are more specific and less general than the IT books you have seen in the past. Our unique business model allows us to bring you more focused information, giving you more of what you need to know, and less of what you don't.

Packt is a modern, yet unique publishing company, which focuses on producing quality, cutting-edge books for communities of developers, administrators, and newbies alike. For more information, please visit our website: www.packtpub.com.

Writing for Packt

We welcome all inquiries from people who are interested in authoring. Book proposals should be sent to author@packtpub.com. If your book idea is still at an early stage and you would like to discuss it first before writing a formal book proposal, contact us; one of our commissioning editors will get in touch with you.

We're not just looking for published authors; if you have strong technical skills but no writing experience, our experienced editors can help you develop a writing career, or simply get some additional reward for your expertise.

Moodle 2.0 E-Learning Course Development

ISBN: 978-1-84951-526-9   Paperback: 344 pages

A complete guide to successful learning using Moodle

1. The new book and ebook edition of the best selling introduction to using Moodle for teaching and e-learning, updated for Moodle 2.0

2. Straightforward coverage of installing and using the Moodle system, suitable for newcomers as well as existing Moodle users who want to get a few tips

3. A unique course-based approach focuses your attention on designing well-structured, interactive, and successful courses

4. Configure site settings, set up the front page, create user accounts, and create courses

Mastering Adobe Captivate 6.0

ISBN: 978-1-84969-244-1   Paperback: 340 pages

Create professional SCORM-compliant e-learning content with Adobe Captivate

1. Step by step tutorial to build three projects including a demonstration, a simulation and a random SCORM-compliant quiz featuring all possible question slides.

2. Enhance your projects by adding interactivity, animations, sound and more

3. Publish your project in a wide variety of formats enabling virtually any desktop and mobile devices to play your e-learning content

4. Deploy your e-Learning content on a SCORM or AICC-compliant LMS

Please check **www.PacktPub.com** for information on our titles

Sakai Courseware Management: The Official Guide

ISBN: 978-1-84719-940-9   Paperback: 504 pages

A comprehensive and pragmatic guide to using, managing, and maintaining Sakai in the real world

1. Covers working with Sakai tools, the administration workspace, and more

2. Includes lots of ideas and best practices for teachers and trainers on using Sakai effectively

3. Create instructional materials and design students' activities

4. A step-by-step approach with practical examples, ample screenshots, and comprehensive content for a wide target audience

WordPress for Education

ISBN: 978-1-84951-820-8   Paperback: 144 pages

Create interactive and engaging e-learning websites with WordPress

1. Develop effective e-learning websites that will engage your students

2. Extend the potential of a classroom website with WordPress plugins

3. Create an interactive social network and course management system to enhance student and instructor communication

Please check **www.PacktPub.com** for information on our titles

CPSIA information can be obtained at www.ICGtesting.com
Printed in the USA
BVOW09s1259240814

363987BV00004B/97/P